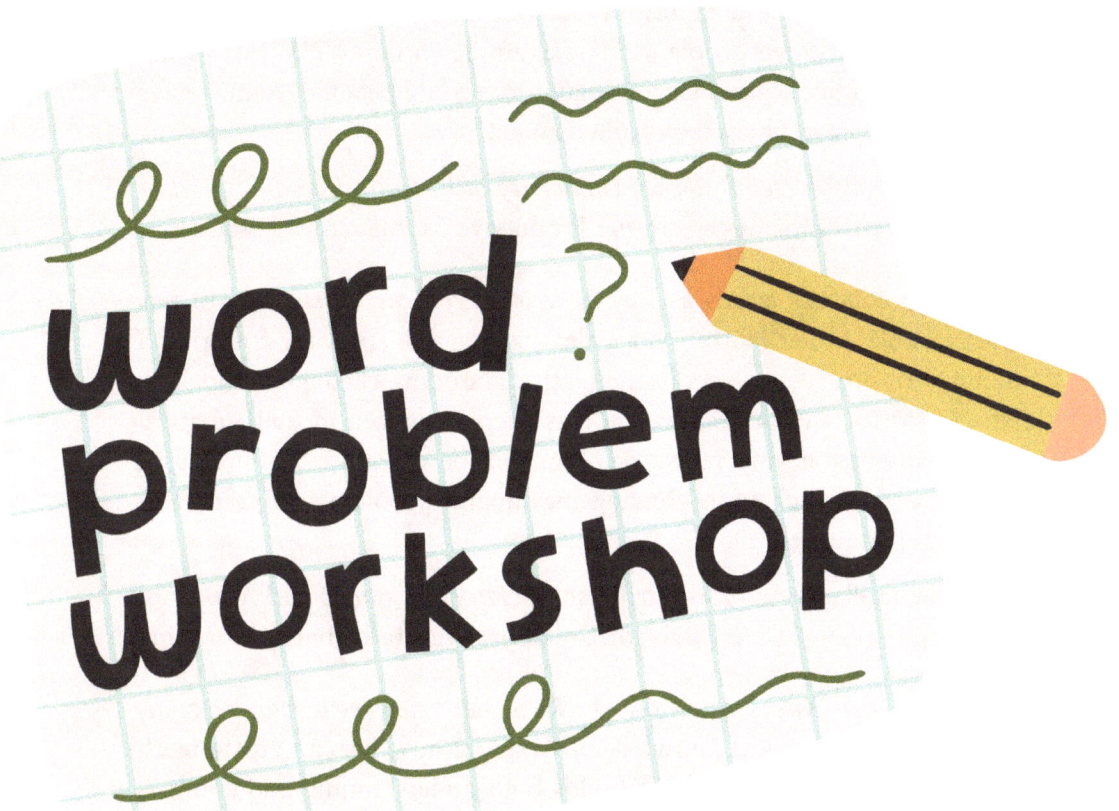

"Mona Iehl's own transformation as a math teacher serves as inspiration and encouragement for teachers who are committed to enriching the mathematics learning experiences of their students. The five steps of the Word Problem Workshop (WPW), along with the norms and practices for building community, provide a guide for creating classrooms where students think, reason, and solve problems. The examples bring WPW to life and help teachers imagine what their own classroom could become. A must have for any elementary teacher ready for a change!"

— **Peg Smith,** *Professor Emerita, University of Pittsburgh and Co-author of* 5 *Practices for Orchestrating Productive Mathematics Discussions*

"Every math educator needs a copy of *Word Problem Workshop*! In this insightful book, Mona Iehl provides clear, actionable steps for fostering a community of problem solvers in the math classroom. Through compelling classroom stories, she showcases students deeply engaged in mathematical reasoning, discussion, and reflection. This will be my go-to resource as a coach supporting teachers in creating meaningful problem-solving experiences for their students!"

— **Nicora Placa,** *Associate Professor at Hunter College and Author of* 6 *Tools for Collaborative Mathematics Coaching*

"In *Word Problem Workshop*, Mona draws on her extensive teaching experience and deep pedagogical knowledge to explore how we can create math classrooms where problem-solving builds both understanding and community. With practical strategies and an emphasis on connection, Mona empowers teachers to shift from rescuing students from struggle to embracing the power of their ideas."

— **Aubrey Wilk,** *Executive Director at Downtown Denver Expeditionary School*

"*Word Problem Workshop* is a must-read for educators looking to deepen and improve their math instruction. Written in an engaging and easy-to-read style, this book offers powerful insights, practical strategies, and plenty of "nudges and nuggets" to help teachers refine their approach in creating a student-centered math classroom in which all students can solve word problems. Whether you're a new or experienced teacher, you'll find motivation and actionable ideas to enhance student learning and confidence in math."

— **Anne Oberdzinski,** *Veteran Educator*

"I've been utilizing *Word Problem Workshop* in my classroom and there is a noticeable difference in how my students think and approach math. *Word Problem Workshop* is essential for both teachers and students."

— **Jimmy Dietmeyer**, *Current Third Grade Teacher*

"In *Word Problem Workshop*, Mona Iehl draws on her extensive classroom experience to offer practical, research-based guidance for building a community of problem solvers. With step-by-step strategies, she equips teachers with the tools to implement her Word Problem Workshop framework, fostering critical thinking, collaboration, and a deep understanding of mathematics. This must-read book empowers educators to create a positive math experience where students embrace problem-solving with confidence and curiosity."

— **Ann Elise Record**, *Consultant and Co-author of* Fluency Doesn't Just Happen with Multiplication and Division

"*Word Problem Workshop* is more than just a teaching resource—it equips educators with practical tools to help students truly engage with and enjoy math. Through real classroom narratives, photos, and step-by-step guidance, Mona Iehl supports teachers at all levels in implementing this student-centered workshop approach. Her candid reflections on mistakes and meaningful math moments make this book an invaluable guide for educators looking to deepen their students' understanding of math."

— **Melanie Doppler**, *Elementary Math Specialist*

"*Word Problem Workshop* is a game-changer for anyone who wants to help their students build healthier relationships with math, think fearlessly, and build unshakable confidence as problem solvers. If you're ready to transform math learning, this is the book you need!"

— **Vanessa Vakharia**, *Author of* Math Therapy: 5 Steps to Help Your Students Overcome Math Trauma and Build a Better Relationship With Math

"*Word Problem Workshop* empowers teachers to transform their classrooms into vibrant spaces where students reason, communicate their thinking, and approach problem-solving with confidence. This daily routine moves beyond key-word hunting and rigid steps, guiding students to make sense of word problem contexts and structures."

— **Kimberly Rimbey**, *Ph.D., Author, Inventor, Consultant, Math Coach, Teacher*

"*Word Problem Workshop* provides a personal coaching experience that will absolutely transform educator and student dispositions towards mathematics. Mona explains the foundational "why" behind the problem-solving approach as well as clear, actionable "how" steps to effectively implement these routines immediately. Thank you, Mona, for making these lofty goals accessible to all of us!"

— **Meghan Hein**, *Second Grade Teacher in San Marcos, CA*

"If you're an educator ready to make math more engaging and meaningful while also building confident problem solvers and a thriving math community then *Word Problem Workshop* is an absolute must-read. With a thoughtful and thorough approach Mona lays out a five-step routine that any teacher can implement, providing all the tools and strategies needed to bring it to life. She truly thinks of everything, and you'll walk away not just inspired but ready to try this approach in your own classroom."

— **Molly Lindhart**, *Fifth Grade Teacher*

"This book outlines a purposeful cycle on how to teach math to keep students engaged, enhancing their understandings, while allowing students to be the leaders of their own learning!!"

— **Amanda Bourne**, *Current Second Grade Teacher*

"Through detailed storytelling and her own deep expertise, Mona brings readers into classrooms where teachers have brought a student-centered math vision to life. An incredible resource for anyone looking to build deep mathematical understanding with young learners!"

— **Maggie Waldner**, *Math Education Consultant, Magpie Math*

"*Word Problem Workshop* provided invaluable insights into creating a student-centered math classroom that can adapt to all grade levels. It empowers students to collaborate, think critically, and solve real-world problems, while encouraging resilience and confidence. By fostering deep mathematical conversations and promoting autonomy, this approach helps students build the skills they need to become lifelong problem solvers."

— **Laura Bird**, *Kindergarten Teacher*

# word problem workshop

**5** Steps to Creating a Classroom of Problem Solvers

Mona Iehl

Routledge
Taylor & Francis Group
NEW YORK AND LONDON

A Stenhouse Book

Illustrations included on the cover and interior by Corn Ahn of Courtney Ahn Designs

First published 2026
by Routledge
605 Third Avenue, New York, NY 10158

and by Routledge
4 Park Square, Milton Park, Abingdon, Oxon, OX14 4RN

*Routledge is an imprint of the Taylor & Francis Group, an informa business*

© 2026 Mona Iehl

The right of Mona Iehl to be identified as author of this work has been asserted in accordance with sections 77 and 78 of the Copyright, Designs and Patents Act 1988.

All rights reserved. No part of this book may be reprinted or reproduced or utilized in any form or by any electronic, mechanical, or other means, now known or hereafter invented, including photocopying and recording, or in any information storage or retrieval system, without permission in writing from the publishers.

*Trademark notice*: Product or corporate names may be trademarks or registered trademarks, and are used only for identification and explanation without intent to infringe.

*Credits:*
Figure 1.11 Strands of Mathematical Proficiency, National Research Council
Figure 1.13 Apple orchard photo by Sara Ramaker
Figure L.4 Ferris wheel photo by Jessica Rueckert
Page 114 Campfire photo by Lily Zandnia

ISBN: 978-1-032-84276-9 (pbk)
ISBN: 978-1-003-51562-3 (ebk)

DOI: 10.4324/9781003515623

Typeset in Sabon Lt Pro
by KnowledgeWorks Global Ltd.

To the problem solvers, big and small—including the three I proudly call mine—the world needs your perspectives.

# Contents

Acknowledgements .................................................................... x

Introduction: Welcome to Word Problem Workshop ............................................. 1

What Is Word Problem Workshop? ................... 8

Step 1: Launch ................................................. 43

Step 2: Grapple .............................................. 57

Step 3: Share .................................................. 91

Step 4: Discuss .............................................. 111

Step 5: Reflect ............................................... 134

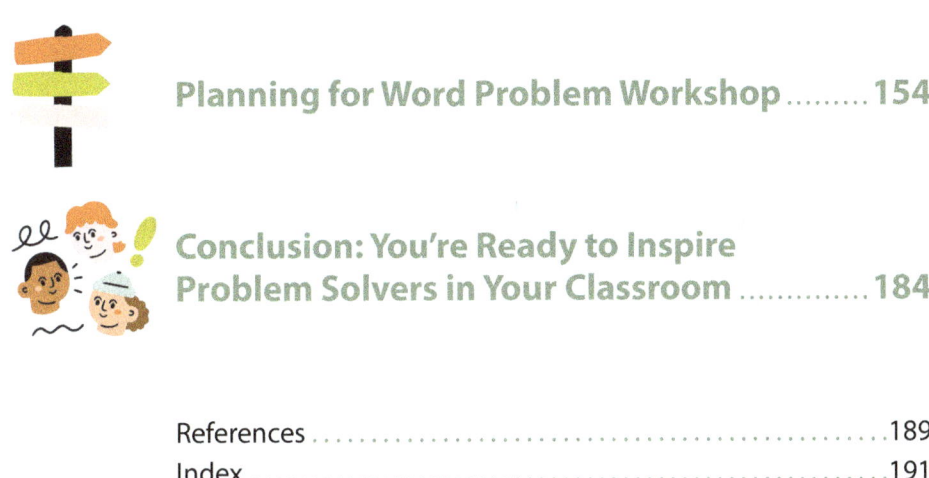

**Planning for Word Problem Workshop** ......... **154**

**Conclusion: You're Ready to Inspire Problem Solvers in Your Classroom** .............. **184**

References ................................................. 189
Index ..................................................... 191

# Acknowledgements

A community is the sum of its pieces. My community, my colleagues, mentors, and students, each shaped my journey. Our collective effort resulted in the learning found in this book. Together, we developed classrooms of problem solvers and inspired a new definition of what it means to "be a mathematician."

None of this is possible without the courageous students, and their families, who embraced the journey of becoming mathematicians and problem solvers in my classroom. You each taught me more than I could ever teach you. You were my kids before I had my own, and I love and thank each of you.

Linda, you showed me how to trust kids to think. The moments we spent in my classroom helped me be a better teacher in the moment and sent me on my own problem-solving path leading me to this moment. Thank you for being my coach, mentor, and one of my best thought partners.

I've been profoundly shaped by the educators and authors whose insights and research have become the foundation of my teaching. I am deeply indebted to Peg Smith and Mary Kay Stein for *5 Practices for Orchestrating Productive Mathematics Discussions*, as well as to Thomas P. Carpenter, Elizabeth Fennema, Megan Loef Franke, Linda Levi, and Susan B. Empson for their work in *Cognitively Guided Instruction*. I'm also grateful to Jo Boaler, Graham Fletcher, Elham Kazemi, Allison Hintz, Jen Munson, John SanGiovanni, and Tracy Johnston Zager for their continued inspiration.

From pre-K to college, in every classroom, I studied the craft of teaching. Every teacher, mentor, and coach I've worked with, observed, or shared a beer with taught me something invaluable. You all helped me write this book, whether you knew it or not.

To my teacher mentors:

Ms. Sheibels, for your multiplication songs—the only glimmer of joy in my early math experiences.

Ms. Guy, for your contagious zest for making fifth grade magical and our special connection.

Mr. Spicer, for showing me how loving and seeing the whole student is really all that matters.

Dr. Marcy Taylor, for showing me that teachers (and college professors) are true badasses.

Dr. Gretchen Papizan, for encouraging me to write.

Leslie Baldacci, for helping me harness my first-year teacher energy and reminding me to eat lunch.

To my teacher besties:

Lauren, my longest grade-level partner and true friend—we've been through it all.

Mark, everyone needs a teacher bestie who builds you up, but keeps you humble like you do for me.

Nora, your steady wisdom and advocacy for kids guided me through countless questions.

Meghan, your social work got me through tough teaching days, and your friendship encourages me every day.

Kristin, my biz-bestie, thank you for being there to celebrate the small things. Your support and thought partnership kept me going.

Beth, Katie, Jody, Susan, Molly, Jenny, Addie, Ann, Franny, and *so* many more Shining Stars—thank you for being my people during both our school's and our own formative years.

To the teachers and leadership at The Academy, thank you for letting me learn alongside each of you as we create a truly magical math community.

To the Bell Elementary community that took me in, trusted me, and listened to my ideas, thank you.

John and Susan at Middle Web, thank you for giving me a place to write before I knew I could write. And John, for the push to write this book. And to Libby Woodfin—your belief in me long before I believed in myself means everything. You set me on this writing journey, and I'll forever cherish you for it.

Kassia, I can't imagine writing this book without you. Your specific and helpful nudges and nuggets pushed me to share the whole story. Thank you isn't enough.

And finally, and most importantly:

Mom, you are the OG problem solver. Your whole life you've persevered joyfully. You're an example of what it means to solve problems in creative ways. I'm so proud to call you my mom.

John, you were the mathematician, and I was the one pretending I wasn't jealous. I hope you know how much I admire you.

Dad, if I could, I'd give you the first copy. You were always so proud.

To all my family and friends, your encouragement and curiosity give me the confidence to share my voice, knowing I'm backed by the people I admire most.

Mike, my partner and teammate, thank you for your unwavering support. You lovingly kept me caffeinated, fed, balanced, and encouraged, allowing me to make the most of every precious moment in this process. I love you.

Rupert, you've been next to me (or inside of me) for every single word. We wrote this together.

Ida, your confidence fuels me.

Warner, your curiosity inspires me.

Although I hope you three don't struggle too much, I hope you find joy in the journey and know that you can solve any problem with what is inside of you. I wrote this for you and your teachers.

# Introduction: Welcome to Word Problem Workshop

I'll never forget the day everything changed in my math teaching. Linda was modeling a lesson in my third-grade classroom that looked nothing like what I thought math lessons were supposed to be. She posed a problem and then stood back, giving students space to explore and think before telling them what to do. I was squirming inside—weren't kids going to get upset and fail? But instead, they came alive with ideas, using what they knew to figure things out and share their thinking. I realized I'd been missing something essential.

Not too long before Linda's lesson, my class was working on addition and subtraction strategies. I demonstrated a few problems at the board while students used white boards to follow along. My engagement was on point and I was sure my students knew what to do. So, I sent them off to answer more questions on their own.

Only seconds into that work time, Robert wasted no time in calling me over, "Ms. Iehl, can you help me?!"

Others joined in. "I can't read this, Ms. Iehl. UGH."

"Why do we have to do this?"

"Can I go to the bathroom?"

"Friends, we just took a bathroom break," I responded, slightly frustrated with the situation. "There are only three problems to solve. Just look at the board and do what I showed you to do." I struggled to quiet the class and re-engage them. I ran around the class between the raised hands doing what I could to help so I didn't lose the attention of the handful of kids that were actually engaged in solving the problem.

If I'm being honest, most math classes resulted in this same type of struggle. I was a fourth-year teacher, and I felt prepared to teach almost every subject—except math. Growing up, I was a confident student, with the exception of math. All through school, I thrived in subjects where I could express my ideas, but in math I relied on memorizing steps without understanding. I was rarely asked to reason or think critically about math. Now as a teacher, I was perpetuating the same problems I faced as a student. I couldn't shake my long-held belief that I just wasn't "a math person."

That belief led me to cling tightly to my scripted curriculum. I often thought, "I can't take risks in my teaching. I have to just stick to the way it's always been because I need them to learn so they don't end up like me." Because I felt insecure in my math knowledge, I was afraid to let students lead. I was worried I wouldn't understand their approach or be able to answer their questions. So, I stayed on script.

"Okay, third graders. Let's go over the answers," I announced, after the frenzy of independent work time, holding the white board marker in one hand and my answer key in the other.

"I'm not done." Sarahi said softly, raising her hand. She wasn't mad, she was worried.

"NO! I'm gonna get a bad grade, again. Please, Ms. Iehl, can we just do this together?" Tyler pleaded.

"Seriously, I hate math!" Sean yelled out, looking to gain support from his peers in the form of laughs.

I saw myself in them; I knew their struggles all too well. But I also knew learning could be meaningful, engaging, and accessible for all my students, I just wasn't sure how to do that in math. My professional development and instructional support focused on all the other subjects, leaving little to no opportunities to confront my own math discomfort and grow as a math teacher.

I knew I wanted more and different for my students. They were inspiring in so many ways, constantly using real-world knowledge to solve problems, both in and out of school. Ciera competed in the National Spelling Bee, Tyler cooked breakfast for his siblings, and Yazmin shared stories of negotiating chores with her five siblings. Sean even started a secret business selling paper trinkets in our classroom. Yet, when faced with a math problem, they froze, struggling to connect all they knew and all they could do with the task at hand.

Not to overstate it, but that lesson Linda modeled in my classroom led to a profound realization for me as a math teacher. I realized that learning math wasn't just a set of skills to reproduce in order to get answers, but rather that mathematicians were critical thinkers and problem solvers. So, I began a journey to transform my math teaching approach.

I learned to trust my students. I reimagined what it meant to be a mathematician in elementary school. I committed to seeing their skills, experiences, and intuition as assets for doing math. Then, I took big risks to let go of my tight control, talk less, and get curious about my students' thinking.

What resulted changed me and my teaching, but most importantly it opened up a world of problem solving for my students. We were no longer beholden to the traditional ways of "doing math," but instead we created a math community that approached problem solving by exploring ideas, thinking deeply about math, and discussing our reasoning. The five steps of Word Problem Workshop helped me transform my own classroom into a place where students could confidently solve problems in collaboration with their community.

*Word Problem Workshop* is a book for all of us who are striving to teach math, and specifically word problems, better than the ways we experienced it as students. This isn't just a strategy book—it's a movement to change the way we teach math. Yes, you'll learn teaching strategies in this book. You'll learn that Word Problem Workshop is a proven five-step routine that allows for problem solving, discussion, and reflection around word problems. But the work doesn't stop there.

Word Problem Workshop is a movement of teachers like us pushing back against the notion of "but we've always done it this way," and standing up to create the math class our students need (and, in some cases, the class we needed as a child). Word Problem Workshop is a safe space where students can embrace mistakes as part of their learning journey, all while solving real-world problems.

We're on a mission to rescue our students from the kind of teaching that demands they rigidly follow the rules and mimic math understanding. Instead this movement encourages us to support students in finding their mathematician voice and in developing a true understanding of mathematics. The strategies for helping students engage in real-world problems don't depend on a certain curriculum or set of standards, but instead rest on the belief that children learn through curiosity and exploration of mathematics. They learn through sharing and discussing their ideas with peers, and through strategic guidance and nudges from teachers. Mathematics is a lens through which to understand our world.

In this book I'll share an approach that worked for me as an elementary school teacher to build my own understanding and engage every child in deeply understanding mathematics. It's a process I've taught to many other teachers who, like us, want to increase their students' engagement and achievement with word problems. You'll learn how to plan, facilitate, and make strong instructional decisions around word problems. Word Problem Workshop leverages students' thinking through daily engagement with real-world, relevant word problems. Intentional time and space are provided for students to engage in problem solving, deepening their understanding, and enhancing their reasoning skills through collaborative math discussions.

## The Roots of Word Problem Workshop

For many of us, our experiences as math learners were shaped by a system that taught us math was rigid, clear-cut, and accessible only to a few. With Word Problem Workshop, we now have the opportunity to re-root ourselves in beliefs that will nourish both our teaching and our students' learning. To lead our young mathematicians with confidence, we must reflect on our own math journeys, examining the beliefs we bring into the classroom and the future we envision for this work. By grounding ourselves in a renewed sense of purpose and understanding, we can empower students to engage fully and take ownership of their math learning.

The work of teaching is deeply personal, and our beliefs and values play an important part in how we show up in our classrooms. Let's take a look at five beliefs that can root our instructional decisions and guide our work in Word Problem Workshop (and beyond!).

## 1. Student-Centered Instruction Promotes Ownership of Learning

If we hold this belief, then we design instruction that gives students the autonomy to solve problems in ways that make sense to them. We avoid forcing students to use any one specific strategy and instead allow them to consider which strategies make sense for solving the problem in front of them. We expose students to new ideas and strategies through collaboration and discussion with peers and support them in deepening their understanding over time. Research indicates that when students themselves are actively engaged in thinking and doing, rather than passively receiving information, they are more invested in their learning and more likely to develop a deeper understanding of mathematical concepts (Michael 2006; Freeman et al. 2014).

## 2. Learning Starts with Student Curiosity and Continues Through Honoring Student Expertise

If we hold this belief, then we make space for students to bring their background knowledge and skills to the learning experiences. We encourage students to use their questions and capabilities to solve problems in their own way, and encourage them to take ownership over the decisions they make along their problem-solving journey.

## 3. Mathematical Discourse Builds Math Understanding and Community

If we hold this belief, then we create a collaborative classroom environment in which students learn to discuss, critique, and build on one another's ideas. We make space for all voices, fostering a sense of belonging and confidence in each student.

## 4. Productive Struggle Is Essential for Deep Learning, as Is Teachers' Support of Students as They Learn

If we hold this belief, then we support students through offering them challenging problems rather than giving them quick solutions. We encourage them to problem solve by trying different approaches, guiding them to build resilience, independence, and a true understanding of math concepts.

### 5. Math Connects Us and Helps Us Make Sense of Our World

If we hold this belief, then we use word problems that reflect real-life contexts that are relevant to our students' lives. We aim to help them see math as a tool for making sense of their world and for engaging with problems that matter to them.

## Let's Get Started By Being Action Takers

If you share some of these beliefs about teaching or even if you're just curious about some of them, this book is for you. I wrote *Word Problem Workshop* for teachers like us who want to make shifts in our classrooms but are unsure of what the next steps might be. I hope the experience of reading this book is like sitting down with a teacher bestie and sharing ideas over lunch. I don't have all the answers figured out and I don't provide a magical recipe for success. My hope is that the ideas and strategies help you build on the work you're already doing in your classroom and help you create a community of capable and confident problem solvers.

In the chapters that follow, I'll walk you through each of the five steps of Word Problem Workshop. Woven throughout each step are ideas for how you'll bring together a community of mathematicians in ways that feel safe and welcoming for all. We will also dive into how to plan and facilitate Word Problem Workshop so that students' ideas and voices drive the learning. I'll show you how your role as the "guide on the side" will be the most fulfilling role you take on as a teacher. We will reflect on what it means to do this work and how we can inspire our students to build the skills of reflection. All of this while remembering that the work you do in your classroom each day and the expertise you hold is the most valuable resource in your classroom.

This work of guiding students to deeper mathematical understanding is easy to start, but never finished. That leaves a door open for you, lifelong learner, to continue to deepen your practice and enhance your skills. I hope that idea excites you to start wherever you are, bringing your assets to the table and being open to new ideas. The work of problem solving is just as much our work as it is our students' and we are in this work together.

## Our Community of Problem Solvers

I hope you will find the feeling of community within the pages of this book—because I wrote with the intention of cheering you and your students on. I also sincerely hope you will share your learning with me. You can find me on social media @hellomonamath or by using the hashtag #WordProblemWorkshop. I have Math Chat podcast episodes organized on my website (monamath.com/podcast) where you can hear me and my guests share even more around the topics in this book. Finally, you can find posts, resources, and a conversation happening at WordProblemWorkshop.com. I encourage you to engage with this community, share your ideas, ask questions, and celebrate your wins. I'm excited by what we can accomplish together as a community by taking these ideas out of the book, into our classrooms, and onto the internet as we grow together.

Finally, as you work your way through the book, you'll see this symbol in the margins of some pages. This is a reminder to visit WordProblemWorkshop.com and download the related resources that will support your work in Word Problem Workshop.

In the words of my student Neo, "Are we going to do a Word Problem Workshop today? PLEASE!! I can't wait any longer!" Let's not wait any longer, let's get to work!

# What Is Word Problem Workshop?

"Friends, let's circle up!" the teacher announces as her third-grade students gather around the perimeter of the rectangular carpet. On the screen in front of them is an image of the teacher's family at a block party. In the photo is a bouncy house and crowds of people in the background.

Ms. Catey launches the day's problem (taken from her math curriculum and slightly tweaked) by telling her students a story about a recent block party in the neighborhood where many of the students live. "Raise your hand if you've been to a block party," she says. Nearly every child's hand goes in the air. "So," she adds, "over the weekend there was a block party on Peterson, some of you may have been there." At this point we've lost a few students, their faces twist into confused looks.

"What's Peterson?" Zavion calls out.

"It's the street I live on," Mariana clarifies.

"Okay, it looks like many of us have been to a block party, right? It is when they close the street and have a party right there in the street. Take a look at the picture up here, what do you notice?" She asks students to notice and then wonder about the picture on the screen.

"I see a bunch of people," Jahmaryion shares.

"Um, that's way too many people in one spot," Lucy chuckles and the rest of the kids laugh in agreement.

"Yeah, I think the lines are gonna be too long, Ms. Catey," John adds. The class laughs more.

"Okay, any wonderings?" Ms. Catey asks, shifting the focus. After a few questions about the number of people and what they might be doing, she reads the problem they'll be solving that day.

> *There were 385 people at the Peterson Block Party on Saturday. More people came on Sunday. There were a total of 733 people who attended the party. How many people came on Sunday?*

After she finishes reading the problem aloud, Ms. Catey asks students to cup their hands around their mouths and whisper to retell the problem. After just a few moments, Ms. Catey sends the students off to grapple at their seats independently. Most are eager and engaged, jumping up and running back to their seats. She bends down and whispers a few words of encouragement to the slower movers still sitting on the carpet. She praises the students that get started immediately by noticing what they do and naming it aloud. "Wow, Zamir is already rereading the problem. Sasha is drawing a model. I see that Zyion has his name on his paper."

Students work for about three minutes before Ms. Catey stops them. "Pause for a moment. I want you to turn and talk about what you're doing and why. Be sure to *listen* to your partner's ideas. Their ideas might help you solve. Go ahead and talk!" Again, she continues to monitor students by listening in while also maintaining a neutral stance. She brings the class back together to see if they're understanding the problem she has given them today. "Shavel, can you share what you and your partner discussed?"

Shavel explains, "Well, we know how many people were there on Saturday… um 385. We don't know how many came on Sunday. We gotta figure that out I think."

"What did he say?" Ms. Catey asks the class to ensure more than just Shavel and his partner understand. A few students repeat what Shavel shared. It is clear that most students understand that they are working to figure out the "missing" number of people that came to the block party on

Sunday. Ms. Catey is pleased they are making sense of the problem and she's ready to move back to independent Grapple Time. She sends the students off to continue their problem solving, now with a better understanding of which students will need some assistance making sense of this problem.

Students get back to work passionately drawing, modeling, and using equations to solve this block party problem. A few students walk over to the supply wall and grab a bin of base-ten blocks and then return to their seats to begin carefully creating a model. Ms. Catey isn't checking anyone's work for the correct answer, but rather, she is intently listening to students and observing them closely. As she circulates around the room, kneeling next to students' tables, she can be heard saying to different students, "Tell me what you're up to," "What are you doing here? How come?" and "What in the problem told you to do that?" In a couple of cases she offers just-in-time scaffolding by asking a more explicit question or suggestion such as, "What part are you struggling with?" "You're having trouble getting started, let's reread the problem together." and "Could you start by drawing what you hear in the problem? Let me reread it for you."

As Ms. Catey listens to her students' ideas, she keeps track of their strategies and the models they create to solve the problem. As she gets a sense of how they are solving, she asks a few students to share their ideas and chooses the order in which they will share them. "Ciera, would you be willing to share your strategy in our discussion in just a moment? Make sure to bring your paper to the meeting area." She gathers the class together and gets ready to facilitate the whole-group student-led discussion.

Students return to the rug sitting again in their rectangular "circle," knee to knee so every child can be seen. Ms. Catey asks Ciera to share while she scribes her model on a piece of large chart paper (Figure 1.1).

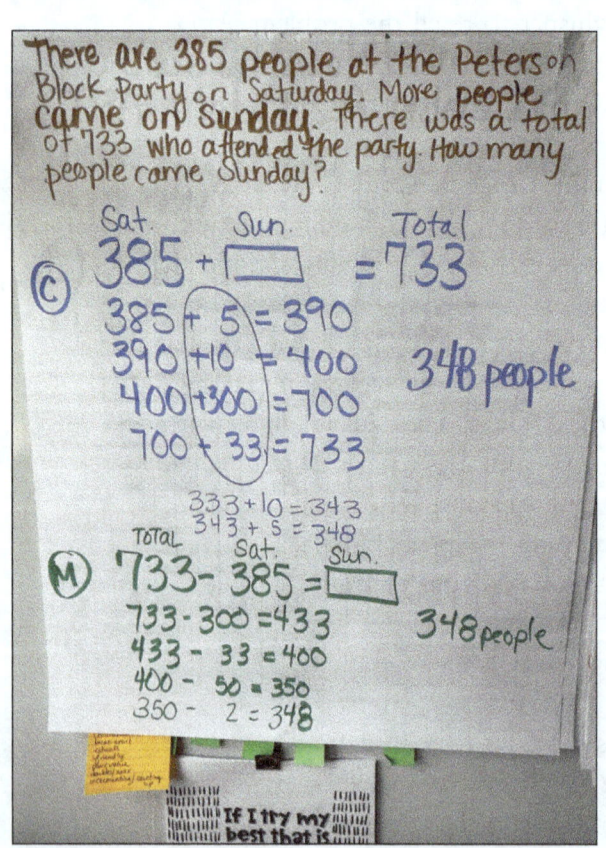

**FIGURE 1.1** The Word Problem Workshop chart created during Step 3 of Word Problem Workshop, the Share.

Students watch closely. Some students tap their heads to show they have a "brain match," while others nod or say "yeah, me too!" to show they are listening and making connections. Another student shares and the teacher scribes their strategies as well. Finally, when the two students have shared, Ms. Catey turns to the whole class.

"We have two different strategies here. I'm curious what you're thinking. Turn and talk to your partner: What do you notice and wonder about these two strategies?" Listening in, she assesses the group's understanding of the strategies.

As the turn and talk ends, Ms. Catey starts the whole-group conversation by calling on a student to share a notice or wonder. Pointing at the chart of student strategies, Laney shares, "I notice Ciera started at 385 and ended at 733." When she's finished, she scans the room and calls on Omarie.

Omarie shares, "I see that one strategy was subtraction and the other was addition." Omarie calls on the next person, Tesha.

She says, "They both have the same answer." Students respond with the sign "I agree with you" in American Sign Language. Ms. Catey pipes up and asks the class to focus on Tesha's comment. "Let's think more about how these strategies are the same, yet different. Who can speak about that?"

Lenox begins. "Well, like Laney said, the first strategy they added up from 385 to 733. In the second strategy they subtracted 385, starting at 733. Um… Alice, you can go next." The conversation continues with students calling on each other, adding to one another's thoughts and asking questions of one another when they are confused.

When Ms. Catey hears a student say something salient she pauses the conversation and says, "What did she say? Yani, what did Tiesha say?" "What did she say, Elijah?" This asking of students to repeat important details is a facilitation move called revoicing, and Ms. Catey uses this move to get a key concept or explanation repeated in as many kids' voices as possible.

The conversation continues and Ms. Catey listens intently. She pauses the conversation occasionally to ask a question. Sometimes her question serves to focus the students' attention on a particular idea. Other times the question nudges students toward a new or deeper understanding of a math concept. Her goal is to get students to do the explaining, to keep their thinking front and center. After about eight minutes of conversation, students begin to get antsy. They take a body break to wiggle and laugh for ten seconds. Sitting back down, Ms. Catey asks them to take two cleansing breaths, and then they are back to the math.

The teacher refocuses them, "We've talked a lot today about the relationship between addition and subtraction and how both students that shared have the correct answer but arrived at it in different ways. We also talked about how we know that there is no one right way to solve a problem. But many of you said this was a subtraction problem, how can you add to subtract? How can they both be right?"

Students' hands shoot up. Ms. Catey reminds students to put their thumb up on their knee and wait their turn to speak, and to remain focused on listening to each other. Students wiggle and bop up and down waiting to be called on. A few students share their understanding of the relationship between addition and subtraction, something they have yet to formally name as a class.

Tucker starts. "Addition and subtraction are related. It's like a fact family. Jackson."

Jackson adds, "I think Tucker means that you can start at the total and subtract or you can add to get the total. It's kinda like 2 + 3 is 5, and that's the same as 5 − 3 is 2."

Ms. Catey nudges, "I think you're on the right track. I wonder if we can prove that both of these methods work by using both strategies with our One More Problem! What will we need to know about these strategies if we are going to use them by ourselves? Turn and talk." Students talk about the strategies by starting at the total number of people at the block party and subtracting to find the missing quantity. Others talk about adding up from what they know to the total number of people. Some discuss writing equations to help them know where the unknown is to decide how to solve.

Ms. Catey wraps up the Discussion by congratulating her students on another day of problem solving and helping each other understand math. She gives them one last task as they wrap up Word Problem Workshop. "Go back to your seats and spend two minutes solving the One More Problem on the board on the back of today's problem. As you walk back to your seat, explain what the relationship between addition and subtract means to someone near you. Off you go!" The students hop up and head back to their seats talking about the relationship. Their One More Problems are collected for Ms. Catey to review in order to plan tomorrow's problem and beyond. The class ends with a math cheer and a promise that they will continue to grow their brains tomorrow. Then it's on to science…

**We can** transform how students approach problem solving word problems by prioritizing just one word problem each day. Through the five steps of Word Problem Workshop, students will use what they know, discuss their mathematical reasoning, and learn from others' perspectives to build a deep understanding of math. As their teacher, you will guide this student-centered process, empowering students to take ownership of their learning.

## Word Problem Workshop

I'll admit that in my early years as a classroom teacher, I did not have the kind of engaging, deep mathematical conversations that I now see in classrooms like Ms. Catey's. Like many new-career teachers, I was focused on getting students to the "correct" answers through demonstrating methods I required them to use. But over time, I learned that math isn't just about getting the right answer. It's about giving students the tools and knowledge they need to become problem solvers, to think critically, and to approach challenges with math confidence.

- 3 to 5 times per week
- 15 to 30 minutes
- 1 to 2 problems per day
- 5 simple steps

As my teaching evolved, I began creating more opportunities for students to apply what they know, solving problems in ways that connect to their own experiences. I realized that math class should be a space where students aren't just following instructions—they should be actively engaging with the material and each other, sharing ideas, discussing solutions, and building a sense of community around learning. This collaborative environment is where true mathematical understanding thrives. This shift led me to develop Word Problem Workshop, which I used successfully in my own classrooms from first through fifth grade and now continue to implement as a math coach supporting teachers across elementary grades.

So, what exactly is Word Problem Workshop? It's a student-centered, community-driven approach to teaching math that fosters critical thinking, encourages productive struggle, and builds resilience—while also creating a classroom environment in which students can work together, learn from each other, and become confident, lifelong problem solvers.

Word Problem Workshop is the best way to engage every child in doing real mathematics each day. It merges the best practices of using real-world problems and engaging in robust math discussions into one predictable routine in which students make sense of mathematics. This daily twenty-ish minute routine can be a stand-alone part of your day or embedded within your math block.

Word Problem Workshop consists of just five steps: Launch, Grapple, Share, Discuss, Reflect. Within each of those steps students are asked to make sense of the word problem, develop strategies for solving, and deepen their broader understanding of mathematics content through problem solving. Word Problem Workshop is an intentional daily routine with powerful impacts on student learning.

Word Problem Workshop is an opportunity to:

- Create a familiar and intentional problem-solving routine
- Invite students to work as mathematicians
- Build a math community
- Facilitate a student-centered approach to teaching mathematics
- Build math proficiency for all students

## Word Problem Workshop Is an Opportunity to Create a Familiar and Intentional Problem-Solving Routine

What do your students expect when they walk into math class? Our daily routine communicates what we value. We want to reinforce for our students that their thinking matters more than answers, that math is a place to make mistakes (and learn from them!), and that within this community we work together to understand math. A simple routine for math class can empower our students to build collective responsibility and a sense of ownership over their learning that leads to math-confident students.

Word Problem Workshop can be a powerful daily experience. However, I've also found success with using Word Problem Workshop four days a week, leaving the fifth day for other structures (such as small groups, fluency centers, etc.). Take a look at Figure 1.2 to see a few sample weekly

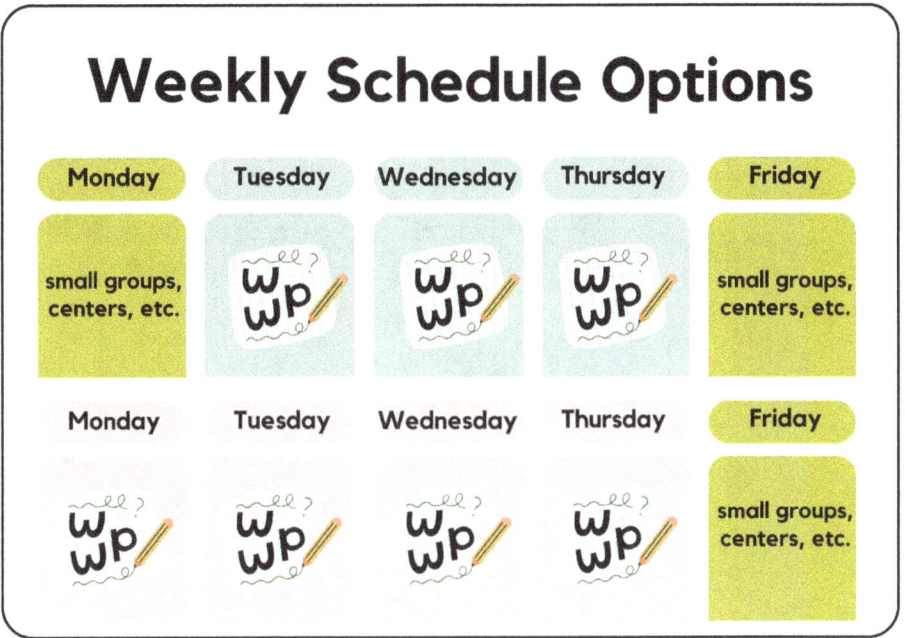

**FIGURE 1.2** When scheduling Word Problem Workshop into your weekly schedule you might opt for three or four days per week instead of daily.

schedules. You'll know your schedule and requirements best; however, creating a routine that is predictable is key to ensuring students know what to expect and get enough practice engaging in problem solving.

Imagine you are in a staff meeting and the idea you contributed to the conversation sparked interest. Your colleagues are agreeing with you and adding onto your idea. How do you feel? Smart, capable, and valued? Your confidence in being a part of the team has grown and now you are being viewed by others as someone with good ideas.

This exact thing happens in our math classrooms when we create a routine.

Word Problem Workshop follows the same five steps each day (Launch, Grapple, Share, Discuss, Reflect). This predictability in structure allows students to feel a sense of safety because they know what to expect. When students feel safe, they are more likely to take risks. For many, taking a risk in math means participating—raising their hand, attempting to do something they aren't sure of, or getting a wrong answer. A predictable and intentional routine allows students to understand that, day in and day out, our math class will uphold the norms of providing safety and valuing in-progress thinking. Over time a predictable routine provides students the space to take risks, expand the ways they participate, and boost their confidence (Figure 1.3).

*What Is Word Problem Workshop?*

**FIGURE 1.3** A routine can help increase students' confidence by creating a safe and supportive environment.

This kind of environment in which strategies and ideas are continually being discussed has benefits both for the person sharing their idea and for those responding to it. In their book, *Choosing to See: A Framework for Equity in the Math Classroom*, Pamela Seda and Kyndall Brown call this concept *Math Status*:

> When a student's problem-solving strategy is shared by another student, this raises the status of the student whose strategy was shared. Raising a student's status helps build confidence. Having students share each other's strategies is also a way to have them include others as experts.
>
> (2021, 28)

The predictable daily routine of Word Problem Workshop builds confident mathematicians.

Word Problem Workshop allows students to make sense and build their understanding over time—a little each day. The routine takes the pressure off packing all the problem solving into "Word Problem Wednesday" or the "application question." With Word Problem Workshop learning is not rushed into memorizing and mimicking the math. A routine lets students learn a bit each day, building onto their understanding and progressing naturally in their learning.

## Routines and Structures to Consider Within Word Problem Workshop

As you develop your Word Problem Workshop routine, you'll need to plan for structures that make efficient use of the time. Many of these structures may already be in place in your classroom throughout the whole day. Nevertheless, attending to these structures specifically within Word Problem Workshop will help students focus their attention and energy on problem solving and reduce distractions.

Consider the structures in your classroom for:

- Movement (forming a circle on the carpet, moving from seats to carpet and vice versa)
- Getting out, using, and caring for materials
- Collaboration (turn and talk, whole-group discussion norms, how to work with a partner)
- Active listening
- Quieting the class and gaining their attention

## When Does Word Problem Workshop Not Work?

Creating a "Word Problem of the Week" structure in which students engage in making sense and solving problems once a week just doesn't work. If students spend four days a week solving problems "the school way" (often through rote practice using a teacher-selected strategy) and then on the fifth day we tell them to solve a problem any way they choose, we send the message that creative and thoughtful problem solving is a "special treat" rather than the main entree. Students in this scenario are often confused and revert back to the strategies and models they've mimicked all week. Worse, they may shut down and do nothing because their skills for trying something new and persisting have not had adequate time to blossom and mature.

Instead, Word Problem Workshop is a routine you can use to shift the approach of how we "do math" in school. We can leave behind the follow-the-leader and mimic-the-steps type of instruction in math and instead open up space to let students' ideas lead. In my classroom we often use a classroom affirmation of, "We have everything inside of us to solve this problem," to remind us that we are all capable of solving problems.

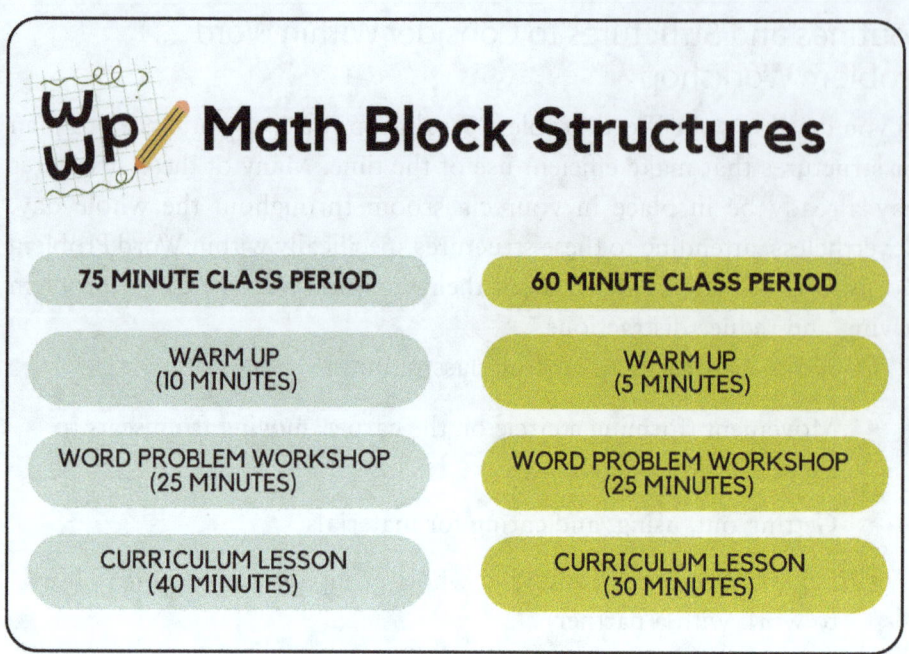

**FIGURE 1.4** Two examples of how Word Problem Workshop might fit into your math block.

I encourage you to consider how you'll integrate Word Problem Workshop into what is already working in your classroom. In Figure 1.4 you'll find examples of how some teachers use Word Problem Workshop in their math block structure. This shouldn't be just another addition to your math block, but rather an intentional shift in how you engage your students in learning mathematics through problem solving. Making the shift takes time. Learning takes time. Giving students time to develop their understanding a little each day means that you'll need to give that time *each day*.

## Word Problem Workshop Is an Opportunity to Become Mathematicians

What is a mathematician? When I ask students this question, they often look at me with their eyes wide, glazed over, and blank. They usually respond with something like, "What are you talking about?" or "This is math," pointing at their book or worksheet. The idea that a mathematician is a real person outside of school or even that *they* are mathematicians is often a new idea for students. If students' only experiences with math look like completing problems in a workbook, then that's what they'll think mathematicians do. Even if this is the kind of math we experienced in school, every teacher I know wants something different, something more impactful for their students. Teachers want students to make connections between school and the world. However, we're often stuck in this routine of "I show you," and "Now you try."

Word Problem Workshop offers an opportunity for students to see themselves as mathematicians. This structure offers students the chance to:

- Examine their own thinking and that of others
- Learn from the reasoning of their peers
- Express mathematical ideas in many forms (visually, symbolically, verbally)
- Make connections to the problems' contexts
- Connect mathematical ideas across problems and contexts

What it really means to be a mathematician is an important question to examine with students. How mathematicians think and act is as important as the content they study. The Standards for Mathematical Practice (Figure 1.5) detail the behaviors of mathematical thinkers, which are vital for all developing young mathematicians, even if your state hasn't officially adopted these as part of your standards. Behaviors that are good practice for all include: making sense of problems, persevering in solving, critiquing the reasoning of others, modeling with mathematics, and more (National Governors Association Center for Best Practices and the Council of Chief State School Officers 2010).

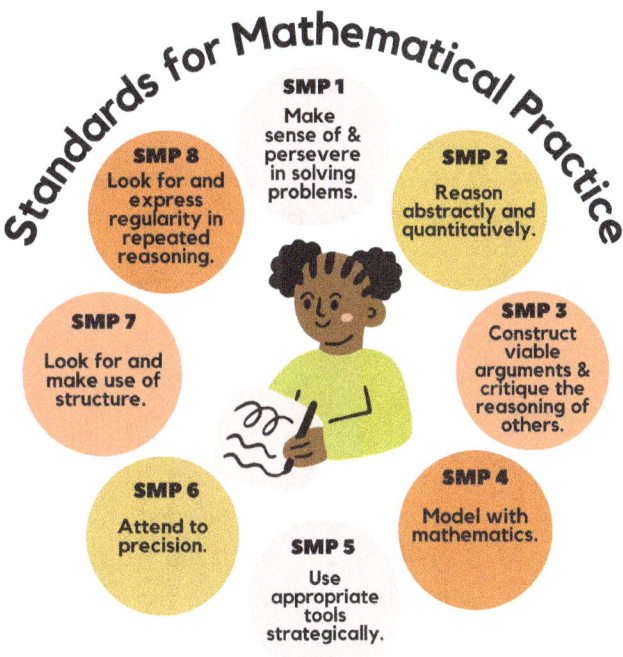

**FIGURE 1.5** The Standards for Mathematical Practice (National Governors Association Center for Best Practices and the Council of Chief State School Officers 2010).

The Standards for Mathematical Practice are integrated into Word Problem Workshop, giving students ample time to practice each and develop these mathematician behaviors with different problem types and math content over time (Figure 1.6).

*What Is Word Problem Workshop?* **19**

| Component of Word Problem Workshop | Standards for Mathematical Practice (SMPs) Integrated into this Component of Word Problem Workshop |
|---|---|
| Launch | SMP 1. Make sense of problems and persevere in solving them |
| Grapple | SMP 1. Make sense of problems and persevere in solving them<br>SMP 2. Reason abstractly and quantitatively<br>SMP 4. Model with mathematics<br>SMP 5. Use appropriate tools strategically<br>SMP 6. Attend to precision |
| Share | SMP 3. Construct viable arguments and critique the reasoning of others<br>SMP 6. Attend to precision<br>SMP 8. Look for and express regularity in repeated reasoning |
| Discuss | SMP 3. Construct viable arguments and critique the reasoning of others<br>SMP 7. Look for and make use of structure<br>SMP 8. Look for and express regularity in repeated reasoning |
| Reflect | SMP 3. Construct viable arguments and critique the reasoning of others |

**FIGURE 1.6** How the Standards for Mathematical Practice (SMPs) connect with the steps of Word Problem Workshop.

## *Word Problem Workshop Is an Opportunity to Create a Math Community*

Just as we thoughtfully build communities of readers and writers in our classrooms, we must also create a community of mathematicians. As a classroom teacher I carefully selected students to be writing partners based on their confidence, interests, and writing skills. I wanted the pairs to be productive, but also for students to feel comfortable getting vulnerable with each other when sharing their writing. I knew these partnerships would take time to develop to their fullest potential. Creating writing partnerships is just one example of how I built our writing community—thoughtful, methodical, and essential to our success. The same is true about the mathematical community we build in our classrooms. In my classroom I looked for ways to build relationships with students and among students. I knew these relationships would be essential for achieving the deep thinking, critical feedback, and productive struggle we would experience together in math.

Let's take a look at a few ways you can build your math community within (and beyond!) Word Problem Workshop.

## Relationships

Relationships with students and among students are vital to a thriving math community that supports the rigorous work of doing and understanding math deeply. The best way we do that is through getting to know one another. I find that simply giving students "talk time" builds relationships best. You can make time for these relationship-building activities during a morning meeting, math time, or anytime when you have a few minutes to focus on being in community with others. The time you invest in students' relationships with you and with each other will pay off across the whole day. Here's one quick activity to get you started!

**Activity: Mix and Mingle to Build Relationships**

Randomly pair students and give a prompt (see the list below). Then, have students mingle. I like to tell them to pretend they are at a fancy party and mingling around like adults. Then I walk around the classroom acting like a fancy adult mingling to really build their buy-in and show them how to get into it. Then, give students a few seconds to mingle and find a new partner with whom to discuss the prompt. This little bit of silly mingling lowers the stress of finding a new partner and increases the likelihood they will just bump into "an old friend I haven't seen in so long" or "Wow! I love your outfit, want to chat?" Possible prompts for discussion include:

- What's your favorite place?
- How do you get to school?
- What do you do after school?
- What's your favorite thing to do at home?
- Talk about your least favorite thing to do.
- Talk about a time you got hurt.
- Talk about your family.
- Do you like math? Why/why not?
- Have you had a good math teacher? What made them good?
- What makes a bad math teacher (no names!)?
- Talk about a time you noticed a pattern (or any math) in the real world.
- Have you ever seen your parents or adult family members using math? If so, what were they doing?

## Math Survey as a Tool for Creating Community and Building Relationships

Math surveys (Figure 1.7) are a valuable and versatile tool for building community and relationships with and among students. Surveys help us gain an understanding of students' mindsets, math histories, and their vision for the future. You can tailor the questions on the survey to be general or specific to a particular issue that comes up in math class. I suggest giving a math survey to kick off the year's community and relationship building and then use it to create your math norms.

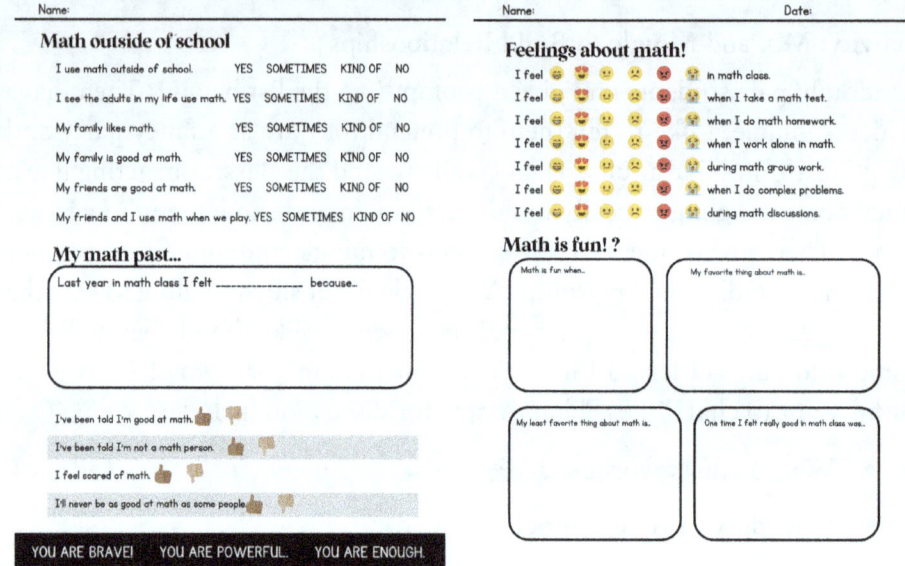

**FIGURE 1.7** Two options of math surveys.

### Tips for Using a Math Survey

- Make a commitment to read each of your students' surveys with an eye toward providing them with the support they need to feel comfortable fully engaging in mathematics. The survey data will help you get to know your students.

- Keep track of the results. Go through the surveys and highlight any details that help you better understand your students. For example, in Figure 1.8 I've highlighted any response that signaled a potentially negative mindset about math. I take note of trends and then plan social-emotional learning lessons to focus on these mindsets and feelings about math.

- Use the survey to make a quick checklist to track day-to-day progress you see in students. Even a simple class list with space to take notes on each student can help you take notes or track progress on individual student goals.

- You can refer back to survey results when you're building relationships with students in math class. For example, in Figure 1.9 a student wrote on their survey that they don't like to explain their thinking. By making a note of this student's feelings, I can find opportunities to build that student's (and others') confidence and find ways to motivate them to share their ideas with others.

- Give this survey multiple times a year. This repetition will allow you to measure how students' math mindsets change over the school year. I suggest giving the survey at the beginning of the year to get to know your students. Then, give the survey again mid-year to compare the results and see how students have grown, as well as noting where they may still lack confidence. At the end of the year, help students celebrate their improvements and give them time to reflect on how they've grown.

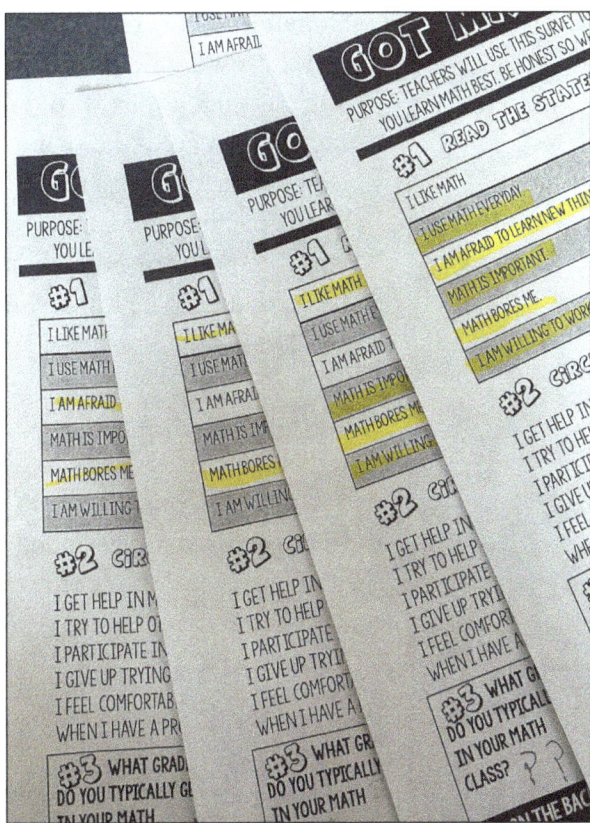

**FIGURE 1.8** After I give a math survey, I go through and highlight students' responses that I want to keep track of.

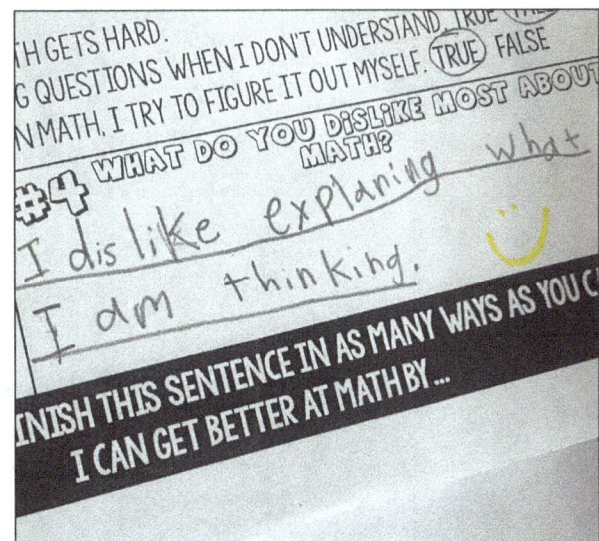

**FIGURE 1.9** A math survey on which a student has written, "I dislike explaining what I am thinking." I keep details like this in mind when working with students during Grapple Time.

*What Is Word Problem Workshop?*

- Share the survey results with all stakeholders! Celebrate your students' growth not only academically, but socially and emotionally. Ask students if they would like to present their progress from the start to the end of the year at their final caregiver-teacher conference. Don't forget to share survey data with administrators—principals, math coaches, and support staff will all appreciate seeing and learning from how you're using math surveys to support every child. Be bold and invite leadership into your classroom for a math mindset lesson or share your survey results with them.

## Math Norms

Creating math norms is a way to develop a shared understanding of expectations and establish boundaries so everyone feels the safety of belonging inside the math classroom. Developing norms alongside your students (rather than just telling them what the norms are) can be a powerful way to build students' investment in living out these norms (Figure 1.10).

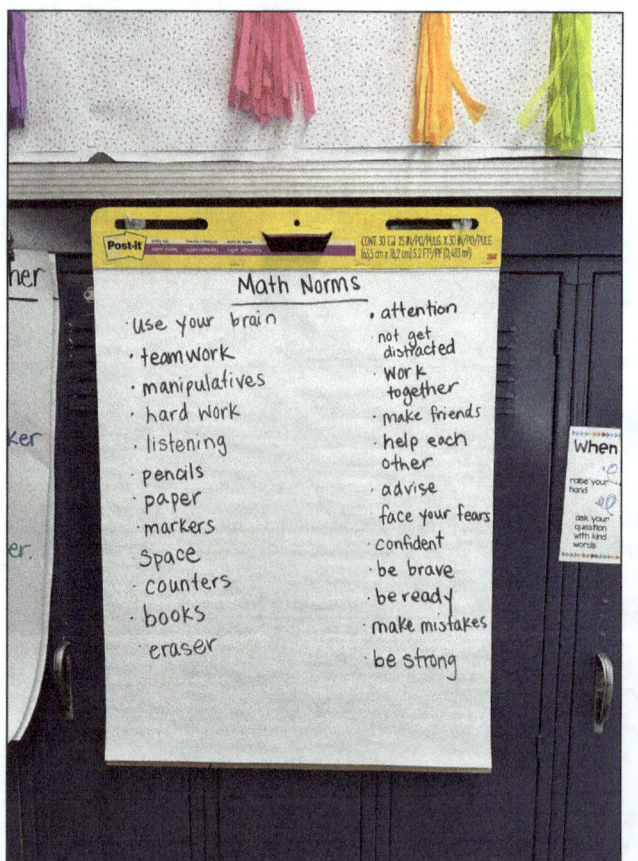 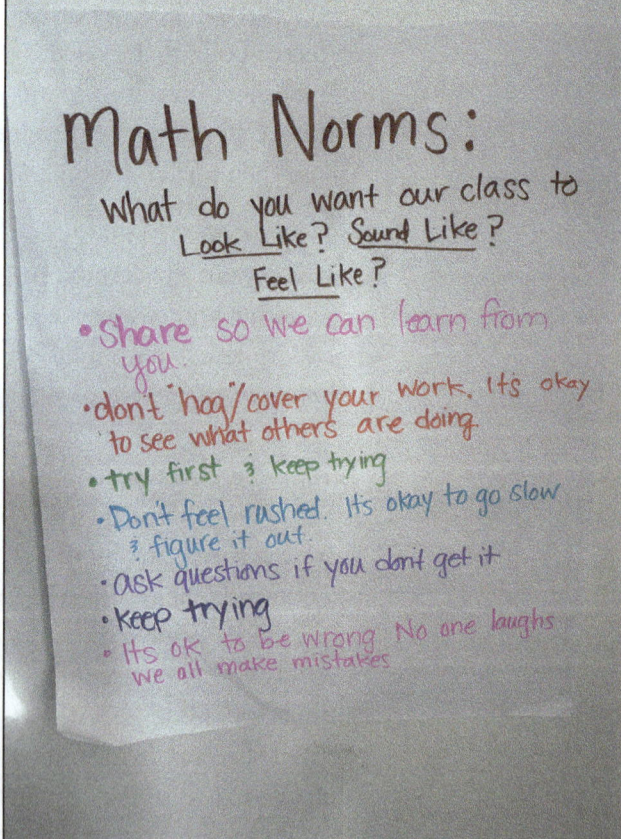

**FIGURE 1.10** A class brainstorm around norms (left) and the norms they wrote after the brainstorm (right).

**Activity: Creating Norms Together**

- **Step 1: Shared experience.** Read a book, watch a video or tell students a story related to a norm you're hoping to build. These experiences show students what is possible. You'll match the topic of the book/video/story to the types of norms you're trying to establish. For example, if you want to think about behavior expectations and emotional regulation, you might read *My Mouth Is a Volcano!* by Julia Cook. Or, if you want to think about productive struggle, consider reading *When Sophie Thinks She Can't* by Molly Bang.

- **Step 2: Brainstorm.** Ask your students, "What do you need in order to do complex work in math class? What do you need from the space, the people, and yourself to support you in taking risks and pushing yourself?" This could be an independent, partner or small-group brainstorm. You can also preview this question by including it in the math survey and presenting the data you gathered for students to reflect on. That might sound like, "When I asked you on the math survey what you need to do complex work in math class, 20% of you said a chance to ask questions; 50% said you need quiet. Do you think we could set some norms based on this?"

- **Step 3: Share.** Have a whole-group conversation to write the norms, condensing the list of needs into some norms everyone can agree on. Discuss each norm by asking, "What does this look like, sound like, and feel like in our class?"

- **Step 4: Use the norms!** Refer to the norms at the start of class, when the class needs a redirection, and as a part of reflection. You might, for example, ask "How did you do today with our norm 'Seek to understand others' thinking?'" The best part of norms is you can change them throughout the year to be responsive to your learners' needs.

## Mindset

A growth mindset is vital to facing challenges in math and combating any anxiety caused by past math traumas. Even students without anxiety or math struggles benefit from strengthening their mindset. For example, my son, who is in first grade, recently told me he was "the worst one on the football field." Of course, I immediately answered with, "Well, how do you get better?" To which he rolled his eyes and said, "Oh… not practicing!"—mocking me, of course. What followed was a conversation about how practice makes progress. We discussed how activities like reading, cartwheels, soccer, snapping your fingers, and yes, football too, all require effort and persistence.

In math class, we can have these same in-the-moment conversations. For instance, when a student gets frustrated, pause to highlight their effort and link their challenge to their mindset. Statements like, "Learning happens when I do hard things," can reframe frustration into persistence. With consistent messages, students begin to embrace challenges as opportunities to learn and grow.

## Reframing Mistakes

Mistakes are not just inevitable—they're essential for learning. Shifting the way students perceive their mistakes can dramatically improve both their mindset and their math understanding. Here are some ways to reframe mistakes in your classroom:

1. **Establish a "no erasing" norm.** Celebrate mistakes by explaining, "Mistakes show us the steps you took to solve the problem." Encourage students to leave their errors visible, as they provide valuable insights into their thinking.

2. **Use mistakes as tools for learning.** Analyze student work that contains errors in order to show how thinking evolves. Ask questions like, "What do you notice about this strategy?" or "How does this help us get closer to the solution?" This process normalizes mistakes as a natural and an important part of learning. "Please, make mistakes, friends—so we can learn more math together!"

3. **Lower the stakes.** The more you celebrate mistakes, the less they feel like a "big deal." Students begin to understand that their mistakes are stepping stones toward improvement. Celebrate with phrases like, "Yay! You made a mistake that led you to a better solution pathway!" or "Mistakes like this show us what to try next—great thinking!" These affirmations transform mistakes into moments of discovery, fostering a safe space for learning and growth.

## Positive Self-Talk

In that same conversation with my son about how to get better at football, we discussed how to replace negative self-talk with positive messages. He compared it to Beyblades, a popular spinning toy.

"There's an evil Beyblade and a superhero Beyblade. The goal is for the superhero to battle the villain and make it burst," he explained.

"But how can that help when you're thinking things like 'I'm bad at this'?" I asked.

"When the Beyblades are battling, each time the superhero hits the villain it says something positive, like 'You're not bad at this—you're learning!' or 'Keep trying—you'll get it!' Every positive thought weakens the villain until it bursts."

In math class, we can encourage students to battle their negative thoughts the same way. Teach them positive phrases to use when negative thoughts pop up:

- "Mistakes help me grow."
- "I can figure this out."
- "I'm getting better every time I try."
- "I'm still learning this, and mistakes are ok."

Over time, students develop their own superhero Beyblade of positivity, ready to combat frustration and self-doubt.

## Word Problem Workshop is a Student-Centered Approach

A student-centered approach to teaching mathematics positions students as the thinkers and doers in the classroom. You might find yourself thinking, "Well of course students are the thinkers and the doers in the classroom. What else would they be doing?" Consider this scenario from my own classroom.

First graders are on the carpet with whiteboards in their laps and markers placed strategically under their crossed legs so they won't be tempted to write until it's time. "Friends, I would like you to look up here at this problem."

> *George has 3 goldfish. He gets 8 more at the carnival. How many goldfish does George have now?*

ME: What should we do first?

STUDENT: See how many goldfish he has now.

ME, FEELING REALLY ENCOURAGED WITH THIS STRONG RESPONSE RIGHT OFF THE BAT: Yes! Let's go ahead and find out how many fish George has now. Let's start at the bigger number and then count up 3 more. Here we go 8 (pointing to my brain) and now, 9 (holding up my pointer finger), 10 (holding up two fingers), and 11 (three fingers up). I added 3 to 8 and got how many?"

STUDENTS PAYING ATTENTION YELL OUT: 11!

**Me:** We could also draw a picture, couldn't we?

**Students:** Yes!

**Me:** That's right. Let's draw circles to represent the fish. I'm going to draw 8 and then 3 more. Then what will we need to do? Andre?"

**Andre:** Um, count.

**Me:** Yes! We could count all of the goldfish or we could just count on starting at 8. Let me draw them and we will try it together.

Reflect for a moment on who was doing the thinking in my first-grade class. Who was doing the math?

As you may have noticed, I was the one doing most of the talking in this example, and I was the one who actually solved the problem. Even though I elicited (minimal) input from students, I was really the one deciding which strategy to use and how I would model it.

I also asked most of the questions. I did a "think aloud" of how I would solve the problem. The questions I asked required students to "fill in the blank," a low-level demand of their thinking. I modeled the problem with my fingers and circles on the board. Both of these models were my construct. Students were hopefully watching and listening while they responded chorally or with their one-word responses, but we can't really be sure. It's clear that in this classroom example, the one doing most of the thinking was me.

If we had a camera in my first-grade classroom in this moment, and we zoomed out from the tight focus on me, we might see what my students were looking at, who was drawing on their whiteboard, who was holding up their own fingers, who was staring out the window, who had their hand raised, who was participating. These behaviors could give us a clue into the engagement of students, and it is likely that students were minimally engaged because I was not asking them to contribute. I was asking them to simply sit and listen as I showed them what to do. This was in my "do as I do" days of teaching.

Word Problem Workshop offers a shift from the teacher doing the heavy lifting to a student-centered approach in which students do the deciding, strategizing, modeling, and describing. In the past I went home exhausted from doing so much explaining while also trying to keep everyone engaged. Now, I tell my students "You should be exhausted from all the work you're doing in math every day."

I want my students to be exhausted from leading their own learning. In *Leaders of Their Own Learning* Ron Berger, Leah Rugen, and Libby Woodfin argue that when students feel ownership over their learning they become more motivated to engage in learning (2014). A student-centered approach allows students to make decisions and take responsibility for their learning, in turn developing independence. This requires an intentional shift on the teacher's part. We move from telling students what to do and how to do it, to facilitating their discovery and exploration of mathematical ideas and skills. The teacher still plays an important role in this kind of learning. It's just that we shift from driving the car to holding the map in the passenger seat.

## Word Problem Workshop Is an Opportunity for Building Math Proficiency

How we define what it means to be "good at math" varies greatly depending on who we ask. I started my career, after two decades of schooling, with the belief that being good at math meant memorizing the study guide well enough that I could reproduce the steps and solve problems on the test to get the A. I started as a young teacher believing that being good at math meant you could follow the directions and get the answers quickly enough to finish the lesson during the math block.

It wasn't until years into my career that I discovered The National Research Council's *Adding It Up* report which was created in response to growing concerns that American children did not have the skills or confidence to do math (2015). Inside this report, math proficiency is depicted as a rope of five interwoven strands: Conceptual Understanding, Strategic Competence, Adaptive Reasoning, Productive Disposition, and Procedural Fluency (Figure 1.11). The report states: "The most important observation we make about these five strands is that they are interwoven and interdependent. This observation has implications for how students acquire mathematical proficiency, how teachers develop that proficiency in their students, and how teachers are educated to achieve that goal (2015, 5).

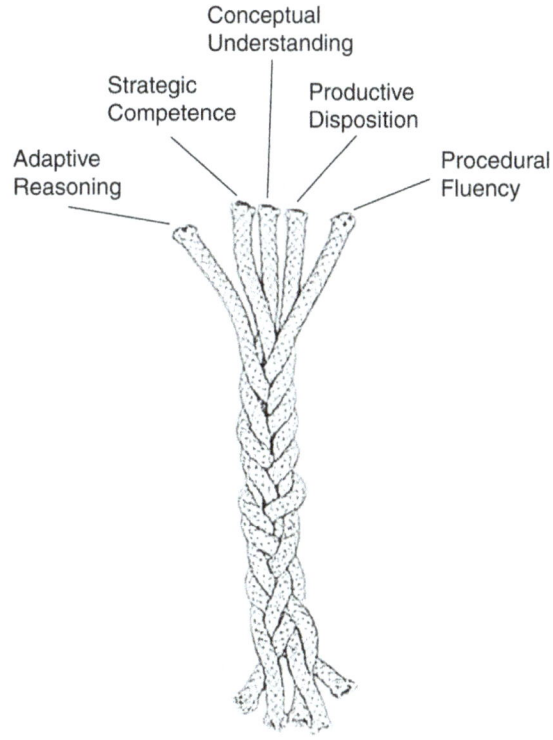

**Intertwined Strands of Proficiency**

**FIGURE 1.11** The five strands of mathematical proficiency (National Research Council 2015).

*What Is Word Problem Workshop?* 29

| Connections Between Word Problem Workshop and the Strands of Mathematical Proficiency | |
|---|---|
| Each step of Word Problem Workshop reinforces a different strand of mathematical proficiency, contributing to well-rounded mathematical understanding. | |
| **Strand of Math Proficiency** | **How Does It Show Up in Word Problem Workshop?** |
| **Conceptual Understanding** <br> Knowing *why* math works the way it does. <br><br> Students understand math concepts and can connect new knowledge to what they already know. | **Grapple:** Students represent mathematical situations in various ways and recognize when certain representations are more useful. <br><br> **Discuss:** Students compare and contrast ideas within their own work and that of others. They not only implement strategies or procedures that make sense but also can explain why they work. |
| **Strategic Competence** <br> The ability to select and apply different strategies, try new approaches, and work through unfamiliar problems. <br><br> Students approach problem solving with creativity and flexibility, essential skills in real-world situations. | **Grapple:** Students choose problem-solving approaches based on prior knowledge, pausing to reflect and recalibrate if needed. They select from a toolbox of strategies, assessing whether their solution pathways are effective. <br><br> **Discuss:** Students justify their problem-solving choices by explaining with words such as, "What I did was ___ because ___," helping peers understand diverse approaches. |
| **Adaptive Reasoning** <br> Understanding and evaluating mathematical arguments, justifying solutions, and critically assessing approaches. This strand is about explaining why strategies work, connecting solutions to the problem, and communicating reasoning. | **Discuss:** Students justify their answers and respond to questions, making sense of their solutions and others' reasoning. They can evaluate reasoning, and give feedback to others. <br><br> **Discuss:** Students analyze and provide feedback on others' strategies. They consider new or revised approaches they might try themselves. |
| **Productive Disposition** <br> Developing the habits and mindset of viewing math as valuable and believing that with diligence they can achieve and make sense of math. | **Grapple:** Students show persistence when faced with challenging word problems, demonstrating a belief in their capacity to solve them. They see math as relevant and useful. <br><br> **Reflect:** Students reflect on their progress, helping them recognize their growth over time and the value in persevering through word problems. |
| **Procedural Fluency** <br> Using procedures accurately, efficiently, and flexibly to solve problems, building from conceptual understanding. Unlike rote memorization, fluency grows from comprehension of concepts and strategic application. | **Launch/Grapple:** Through repeated problem-solving experiences, students choose efficient strategies based on understanding. This approach helps them build procedural fluency. <br><br> **Reflect:** By reflecting on the efficiency and accuracy of their methods, students identify strategies that build fluency and accuracy over time. |

**FIGURE 1.12** Connections between Word Problem Workshop and the strands of mathematical proficiency.

Word Problem Workshop offers a way to integrate each strand of math proficiency into our daily problem-solving time with students (Figure 1.12). Students work to develop conceptual understanding, strategic competency, and adaptive reasoning as they explore solution pathways of the daily word problems. Over time students' productive disposition will shift toward finding joy and fulfillment through grappling with and discussing their ideas with peers. Finally, procedural fluency grows from conceptual understanding and will develop as students build more efficient and effective strategies.

In my own classroom I've found it useful to teach in ways that integrate the five strands of mathematical proficiency. If the focus is on just conceptual understanding and then later on how to reason, the learning is disjointed. We draw on all of these strands of math proficiency as we tackle new problems or choose which strategy is best for which problem. The strands are strongest when they are working together.

In Word Problem Workshop we give students a word problem they are excited to solve and allow them to think strategically, finding ways to solve and then discussing their reasoning with others. The process guides students through integrated practice that, over time, develops their mathematical proficiency.

## The Five Steps of Word Problem Workshop

Let's take a brief look at each of the five steps of Word Problem Workshop. While we will dig deeply into each of the steps in the chapters to come, here we'll take a glimpse into how all five steps come together.

### Step 1: Launch

"Have you ever been to an apple orchard? Think in your mind about what it looks like," second-grade teacher Abby says with excitement in her voice, like she's reminding students of a trip to Disneyland. She displays a photo of an apple orchard on the board (Figure 1.13). Abby wants to make sure that, regardless of their prior experience with apple orchards, all students have a sense of the context for this problem.

Some students start whispering excitedly, while others look confused and are shaking their heads no.

"If you haven't been to an apple orchard, it is okay. In fact, I never visited one myself until I was much older than you. Where I grew up in Michigan there were several orchards nearby, but here in Chicago there aren't any. You have to travel outside of the city to go to an apple orchard because it is a large

**FIGURE 1.13** A photo of an apple orchard. Using a photo to help students make connections to the context is a frequently used strategy during the Launch.

field of apple trees. Rows and rows and rows of apple trees." Abby gestures again to the photo as she says "rows and rows of apple trees."

Abby is launching a Word Problem Workshop problem with her second-grade class. She's chosen this context because it aligns with their social studies unit about understanding the community they live in and comparing it to other communities. The "rows and rows of apple trees" aspect of this problem also aligns with Abby's mathematical goal of laying the foundation for understanding the relationship between multiplication and division.

She continues, "Alright, let me tell you about something that's really important about apple orchards. When talking with an apple farmer, she explained to me that when they plant the apple trees, they space out the apple trees to leave room for them to grow bigger. So, they have to give the trees space and not plant them too close together. This means she can only put eight trees in each row. Now the farmer has forty-eight apple trees to plant in her orchard. She and I were talking about how she could figure out how many rows of trees she will have if she puts eight trees in each row. Can you help her? Look up here where I wrote the problem out for us" (Figure 1.14).

Most students are engaged, though a few seem distracted or confused. Some are already solving—counting on their fingers or quietly discussing ideas with a friend. While some are eager to dive in, others are still warming up to the challenge.

Abby reads the problem as students look and listen. Then, she covers the words and says, "I want you to get a picture of this in your mind. I'm going to read it again and you paint a picture in your mind. Maybe it's even a moving picture—like a movie where you're watching how the farmer will plant these forty-eight apple trees. Ready?"

She reads the problem again as students imagine. "Okay, now it's time for you to retell the problem. Turn to your elbow partner and take turns retelling the problem. If you forget the numbers you can look up here, but challenge yourself to retell, not reread. Go ahead."

For nearly a minute students retell the problem to their partners. Abby listens in and notes who has a strong understanding of the problem and who is still working to understand it. As the chatter comes to a close, Abby thoughtfully pulls them back before students' conversations start to wander off task.

**FIGURE 1.14** The apple tree problem Abby displays during the Launch.

"Alright, I think we're ready to solve. One last question. Will the farmer plant more or less than forty-eight rows of apple trees? Show me with your hands. Will there be more than forty-eight apple trees in each row (puts her hands wide in front of her) or less than forty-eight apple trees in each row (narrows her hands close together in front of her chest). I see Yadiel showing me a signal, I see Brianna, Nova, and Lily. Okay! Let's solve this problem."

Abby reminds students that they will need to grapple and show their thinking. Then, she sends them off to their work spaces to solve.

The Launch is the important first step of Word Problem Workshop where we read the problem, understand the context, and ensure students are ready to solve. While the Launch may look different in kindergarten compared to fifth grade, the goal remains the same—to engage students with the problem and prepare them for solving.

## Step 2: Grapple

Abby's twenty-four second graders stand up from the carpet where they've just been *launched* into the problem with a sense of purpose. Many students walk back to their seats with a look of determination, although a few seem a little uncertain. Each table captain stops at the supply shelf to grab a bin of manipulatives and places them on their table.

Cal sits down at his seat, grabs his pencil, and starts drawing circles. He draws eight circles on his paper.

Rihanna is drawing forty-eight tally marks in rows of eight. She draws eight tallies in a row, then moves down and draws eight more. At the end of each row she writes 8, 16, 24, and so on until she reaches 48.

Three kids sitting at the same table are a bit stumped about where to start—staring blankly at their papers, pencils lying on the table untouched. One of these students takes out the Unifix cubes and starts counting out forty-eight cubes by pulling out four sticks of ten and then stops.

Abby is scanning the room, watching as some students get started, taking note of who is stalled. We call this move scanning because the teacher scans the room much in the same way as a lifeguard scans a pool on a hot summer day, ensuring they have a lay of the pool and how the swimmers are doing. Abby makes the decision to move toward the table of three students who look stuck.

"What's going on here, friends?" she asks. She's met with blank stares and a couple of shrugs. "Okay, how about I reread the problem. You get a movie in your mind and then be ready to tell me how many apple trees the farmer has to plant. Okay, ready? I'm going to read it," Abby says to the table. Abby rereads the problem to the three students. Then she prompts, "How many apple trees does the farmer need to plant?"

"Forty-eight!" one boy says excitedly.

"Okay. Do you all agree?" Abby asks.

The three students all nod their heads.

"Place your finger on the forty-eight in the problem," Abby says.

Now that all the students have found the forty-eight in the problem, Abby asks, "What does the farmer need to do with the forty-eight trees?"

"He plants them in rows," another boy shares.

Abby waits to see if anyone else has something to add. The kids are all looking at her and waiting for her to explain to them what to do. She stays strong, and asks them if they have any other ideas of what the farmer does with the forty-eight apple trees. "Go back to the problem if you need to," she reminds them.

In this moment, it would have been very easy for Abby to tell these students that they needed to put the forty-eight trees into rows of eight and then suggest a strategy for doing so. However, Abby knows how important it is for *students* to make sense of problems and find solution pathways that make sense to them. She is using this time to assess students' current understanding of the problem and nudge them toward making decisions in their solving.

"Okay, friends. You told me the farmer has forty-eight apple trees to plant into rows. I want you to keep going. I'm going to walk around and then I'll check back on you." Then she moves on to observe another table.

Now that all students are working on solving, Abby walks the room to get a feel for students' understandings and strategies. When she planned this problem, Abby forecasted what she thought her kids might do when solving (Figure 1.15). Notice that she forecasted that students would draw trees by ones, putting eight in each

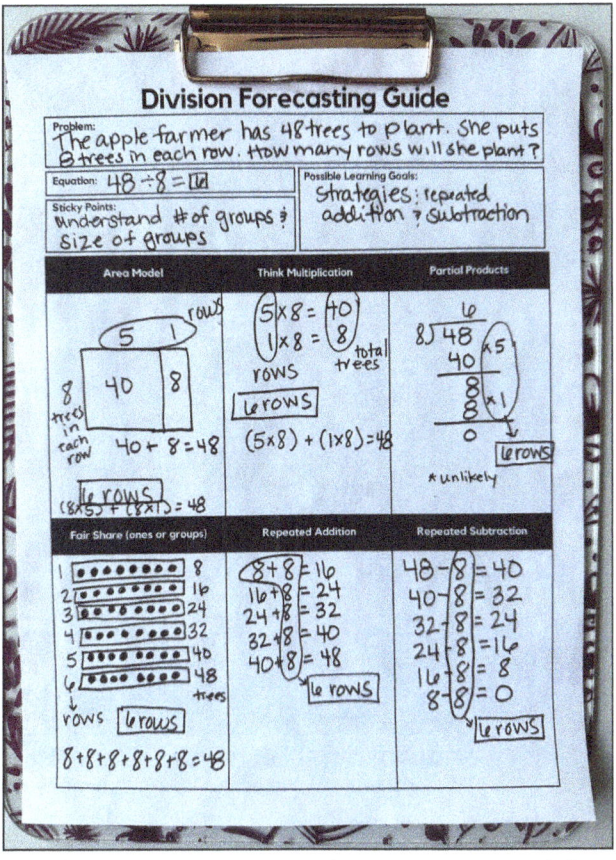

**FIGURE 1.15** The teacher plans for Word Problem Workshop by completing the Forecasting Guide and using it to track observations during Grapple Time.

row and stopping when they counted forty-eight and then go back to count the number of rows. They might also get out forty-eight cubes and subtract groups of eight as they "plant" each row of eight. Abby's second graders are not yet multiplying, but have experiences with multiplication and division problem types. They typically use counting strategies to solve and model these problems with manipulatives and drawings.

There may also be a few students who can count by eights to forty-eight, keeping track of the number of eights they count on their fingers. Some might even use a number line to show their skip counting and the number of jumps. As Abby walks, she assesses where students currently are in their thinking, notices which strategies she anticipated are being used, and which students' work could help bring her learning targets to life during the discussion.

A few tables over, a student is busy using Unifix cubes to create the rows of eight (Figure 1.16). Although there are a lot of cubes spread out

**FIGURE 1.16** To solve the apple tree problem, a student turns sticks of ten cubes into sticks of eight and then uses the "spares" to make the final group of eight.

across the table, the student is using them appropriately, breaking down the sticks of ten and placing the remaining groups of eight on her desk in a row. Then, she attaches the remaining four groups of two cubes together (the "spares" from turning sticks of ten into sticks of eight). Abby wanders over to observe silently. The student doesn't even look up, they just keep working.

Notably this "not even looking up" is a common reaction from students immersed in Word Problem Workshop. They know this is their time to work through the problem and try things out. At this moment, they do not appeal to Abby for help or to confirm their answers. Instead, they continue working by using math tools or drawing their ideas on their paper. When the timer rings they quickly clean up and listen for Abby to call them to the rug for the Share.

Grapple Time is a time for students to problem solve with focused effort. Although some students may be a bit confused or unsure as they get started, it is important to give them an opportunity to take problem-solving action rather than jump in to rescue them immediately. Students will often engage in productive struggle during this time as they try different approaches. While students are grappling with the word problem of the day, teachers are using Grapple Time to shape their own understanding of students' current strategies and consider how to structure a follow-up discussion that will move students' thinking forward.

## Step 3: Share

"Let's have Cece and Oliver bring their work to the circle," Abby announces.

A few students turn to the "sharers" and smile or say good job. One student sighs loudly, clearly disappointed it's not their day to share. As the students move to the carpet, Abby stands next to that student and says, "The way you solved the problem was interesting too. Today I want you to listen carefully to how Cece solved and compare how it's the same and different to what you did. I'll be calling on you to speak in the Discussion." Assigning the disappointed child a "role" in the Discussion gives this student the encouragement they need to engage during the Share and also takes the focus off not being "picked."

Students sit down on the carpet, ready to learn from the first sharer. Abby says, "Cece, tell us how you solved. Tell us what you did and why you did it."

Cece starts by explaining step by step how she solved the apple tree problem, pausing after each step to explain why she did it. Abby scribes her strategy on the chart paper at the front of the meeting area. She refers to Cece's paper as needed to be sure she represents it true to Cece's work. As Cece talks, Abby is careful to only ask for clarification and not take over the conversation, keeping Cece's voice at the center. The goal is to honor Cece's ideas and learn from her.

"Okay. So, how many rows of apple trees did the farmer plant?" Abby asks Cece.

Cece responds in a full sentence. "The farmer planted six rows of apple trees."

"And what is the equation you wrote to match your work?" Abby asks.

"I did 48 minus 8 minus 8 minus 8 minus 8 minus 8 minus 8 equals 0. And to match the equation that goes with the problem I wrote 48 divided by 8 equals mystery box." Cece responds.

"Thank you for sharing your thinking, Cece. Friends, let's celebrate Cece with two claps and two snaps. Here we go..." Next Abby asks Oliver to share his ideas in the same way. Once Abby scribes Oliver's model and he describes his strategy, Abby asks the class to examine the two strategies and models (Figure 1.17).

## Step 4: Discuss

Abby asks students to turn and talk about what they notice and wonder about Cece and Oliver's ideas. Abby listens in to the turn and talks, considering what she hears and who she will call on to start the discussion. She takes a mental note of anything important or related to the intended goals to be sure to circle back to those ideas during the discussion.

"Yazmin, you start us off," Abby announces after she's called the students back from the turn and talk. Yazmin describes her notice and then calls on Rose. Rose shares her idea and then calls on Gus. Gus shares and calls on Timothy.

**FIGURE 1.17** During the Share, Abby scribes Cece and Oliver's strategies.

This goes on until twelve students have shared. Abby has established this structure where students call on one another after they've finished sharing. It allows students to feel ownership over the discussion and increases engagement. As students share, Abby is listening intently but also making space for every child to participate and share any idea they might have.

The conversation starts to stall out a bit as students begin to repeat ideas that have been shared like, "They both have the same answer," "She subtracted and he added," "They did it differently but got the same equation for the problem" and so on.

Abby brings the conversation back by prompting students to return to an idea related to her learning goal: "Let's go back to what Rose said: 'Cece subtracted, Oliver added, but they both have a division equation for the problem.' Can you look at their work and see if you can figure out what's going on? Work it out with your partner in a turn and talk. Go ahead."

Students talk, point, think, and some pause to reconsider.

Abby calls the class back together, "Okay. Let's discuss. How do they both have a division equation, but Oliver added and Cece subtracted? Nora, what do you think?" During the turn and talk, Abby listened to Nora and

Katie discuss how "division is repeated subtraction" and "addition is like multiplication." She's hopeful this will kick off a conversation that will lead to a generalization or conjecture about division.

"Division is just subtracting the same amount over and over again. It's kind of like how if you add 4 plus 4 plus 4 plus 4 plus 4 (five times) then it is 4 times 5. They are both 20. So, division is just subtracting over and over again until you have zero." Nora explains.

Abby quickly says, "What did she say? Turner, what did she say?" Turner revoices what Nora explained. Abby again asks, "Ryan, what did she say?" He revoices. Abby asks the class, "Do you agree? Is one way to think about division subtracting over and over again? Repeated subtraction? Hold up a thumb if you agree. Point it down if you disagree."

Students' thumbs are mostly up, with a few looking confused and swaying between up and down, while two students are adamantly pointing their thumbs down.

Abby thinks. Her goal was to get students to notice *how* students solved this division problem, but this discussion is really taking a turn toward explaining and conjecturing about what division is and how it works. Abby decides to take it there and see if students can develop a beginning understanding of the definition of division.

"Okay, I would like us to try to explain what division is by looking closely and discussing what Cece and Oliver did to solve this problem. Who can explain how Oliver divided when he added the rows of eight apple trees together?" The discussion goes on for a few more minutes with students sharing their reasoning, using the strategies on the chart as their evidence.

On this day in Word Problem Workshop, like every day, the Discussion allows students to lead by sharing their reasoning, critiquing the reasoning of others and broadening their perspectives through listening to others' justifications. The teacher scribes two to three students' strategies so all can see. Then, the teacher facilitates a student-led discussion of those strategies. It is during this time that students often make connections between ideas and strategies, digging into explaining their reasoning. I've found that it is this discussion time that really pushes students beyond just solving the problem to thinking critically about the mathematical understanding through noticing patterns and connections between models, strategies, and problems.

## Step 5: Reflect

Abby is ready to wrap up the discussion and send students off to reflect. She says, "Okay, friends. I want you to think about the division definition

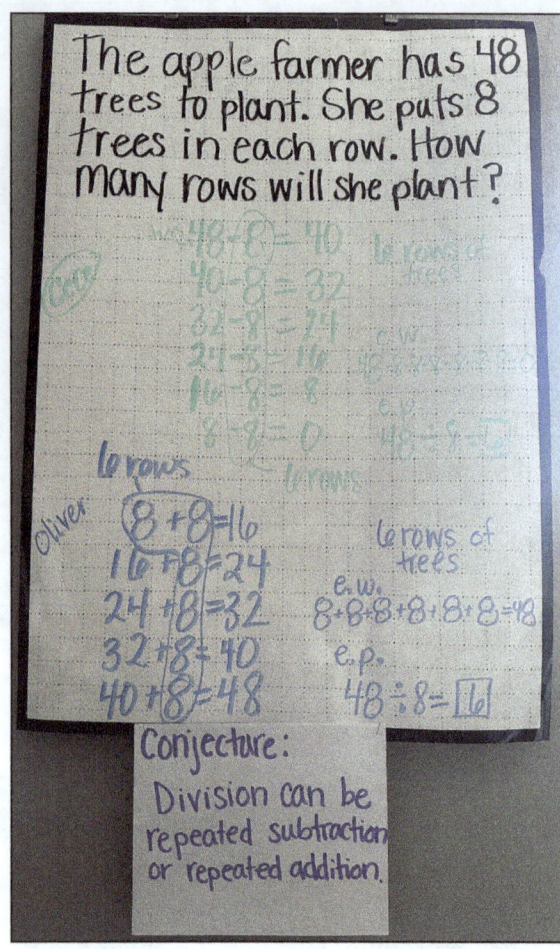

**FIGURE 1.18** The completed Word Problem Workshop chart including the problem, scribed strategies from two students and the class's agreed-upon conjecture.

we came up with today." She points to the definition the class wrote together on the chart (Figure 1.18).

"We are going to solve another problem. I want you to use what you learned today during the Discussion to solve this new problem. Here is the problem." Abby points to the board where she has another problem about the apple orchard.

*The farmer has a different type of apple tree that needs even more space to grow. She can only put 6 apple trees in each row. She has 48 trees to plant. How many rows will she plant?*

Abby chose this problem to assess how students can apply the ideas that came up about division in the discussion to a similar problem. Additionally, Abby will use this problem to assess how students did with improving their model and equation after the discussion, comparing it to what they did in the first problem.

Finally, she asks students to fill out their two sentence reflection—a routine they do each day. "At the bottom of your reflection problem, write two sentences about something you noticed, heard, or learned today." Students drop their completed problems into the pink, orange, or green bin and take out their afternoon snack. Abby uses the bins to help students self-reflect on their understanding. Students place their paper into the bin to reflect "I got it" (green bin), "I'm still figuring this out" (orange bin) or "I'm confused and need some help" (pink bin) Then, Abby marks on the edge of the paper with a marker to indicate which bin students put their paper in. This helps her informally assess students' confidence with solving the problem.

At the end of Word Problem Workshop, it's essential to dedicate a few moments for reflection. Students are given time to think about what they encountered during the Grapple and the Discussion, which helps solidify their learning and deepen their understanding of the strategies they explored. This reflection time allows students to solve a similar problem, apply new skills, or even set goals and track their progress. By doing so, students are better prepared to apply their learning to future challenges. Reflection is also crucial for teachers, who can use this time to assess students' thinking and application of new skills, as well as to plan next steps for instruction.

## Be an Action Taker

### First Steps

1. Reflect on your daily and weekly schedule. Find time for Word Problem Workshop three to five times per week for fifteen to thirty minutes. As you're learning this method it may take longer, but after a few weeks your routines will be established and the workshop will move more efficiently.

2. Lay the groundwork by co-creating a definition with your students of what a mathematician is, and what they do.

3. Cultivate a strong community of mathematicians by selecting one community- and relationship-building activity (i.e., giving a math survey, creating class math norms, practicing positive self-talk, or discussing how to reframe mistakes) to try each week as you begin incorporating Word Problem Workshop.

### Ready to Run

1. Dive in, this is a learning-by-doing book! Give Word Problem Workshop a go. The best way to learn is by trying it out and then spending a few minutes reflecting on what went well and what questions you still have.

2. Reflect on the story of Abby's second-grade Word Problem Workshop in this chapter. Compare and contrast this workshop with a typical math lesson. Develop a question or wonder related to Abby's Word Problem Workshop.

3. Locate the online resources for this book and download them. Anytime you see this symbol as you read, you'll know there is a corresponding resource in the online materials at www.WordProblemWorkshop.com. Inside the resources for this chapter you'll find links to videos of Word Problem Workshop in action.

# Step 1: Launch

Ms. Leslie projects a picture of the school's gym teacher, a silly guy who enjoys playful banter. She asks the students to turn and talk about what they know about Mr. Reid. There's a lively discussion about his healthy habits, working out, and his active lifestyle. The teacher then shows a picture of a fitness app that tracks calories burned. She shows students how people can track their calories in an app and asks students to share what they know. Once students have explained what it means to track calories and exercise, it's time for the teacher to tell the story of the problem.

　　The teacher turns to the students and explains that on Monday Mr. Reid ate 2,453 calories. Giggles and "oohhs" come from the students—they are eating it up (pun intended). Then she goes on to explain that he biked to school that morning, burning 328 calories. Students start jotting down the numbers and she reminds them to just listen to the story. "Then," Ms. Leslie continues, "after school that Monday, he goes for a three-mile run." She explains that three miles is like running from their school to the nearby park and back. "For each of those miles Mr. Reid ran, he burned 281 calories. Let's figure how many calories Mr. Reid did *not* burn off with his exercise, shall we?" The excited crowd of kids exclaims, "YES!"

The teacher is a bit surprised at the level of engagement, but she knows this multi-step problem will be complex to solve, so she wants to make sure they really understand the context. She asks students to explain the problem by retelling it to their partner. During the retell Ms. Leslie displays the written problem and hands out a worksheet with the problem printed at the top.

She calls the students back together after their turn and talk and asks them, "Did Mr. Reid's three-mile run burn more, less, or exactly 281 calories?" Students flash a hand signal, indicating their thoughts.

Lastly, the teacher reminds students of their focus, "Friends, I want you to remember that this month we are working on having courage in math. Showing our thinking on paper and speaking up in math discussions can be intimidating. Today I'm going to look for people showing courage to give a shout out to, because mathematicians show courage when explaining their reasoning and justifying it with their math work. Are you ready to solve? Let's get to it."

Students grab their pencils and immediately start solving. Looking around, everyone except one student is writing something on their paper.

> **We can** launch word problems in ways that honor students' expertise and prepare them to take their first steps into problem solving. The Launch offers teachers valuable insights into students' understandings that can help them support all students.

## Launching Prepares Students to Solve

The Launch sets the stage for your students to tackle the problem. In just a few powerful minutes, you'll help students wrap their heads around the context of the problem and be prepared to take the first step toward their solution pathway.

The Launch part of Word Problem Workshop typically lasts three to five minutes. Resist the urge to teach during this time. Your role, in these first few minutes, is to help your students make sense of the context of the word problem. I like to think of myself as the storyteller during this time, capturing the hearts and minds of each learner through my words. You don't have to imagine yourself as an old witch telling a story around a cauldron luring children near, but you *do* want to use teacher moves in the Launch that will build excitement for solving.

The teacher moves in the Launch draw on students' background knowledge and expertise. You'll help them notice and wonder about the context of the problem. Then, you'll ask them to consider their first step into the problem-solving pathway and check their understanding. You might even give a little pep talk to help students go into problem solving with confidence and courage so that they are prepared to grapple.

### Goals of the Launch

- Build understanding of the story context in the problem
- Give students the opportunity to read the problem multiple times for clarity
- Spark engagement and investment in solving the problem
- Consider the relative "size" of the answer

## Building Independence with the Launch

Comprehending the problem is something that stands in the way of many students successfully solving word problems. It is vital to make the Launch a daily routine so students get practice reading a problem, thinking about the context, and asking themselves questions about the problem. Before long, reading the problem multiple times and considering the context of the story will become a practice students do independently when they encounter word problems.

The Launch can look many different ways and it can be crafted to fit the needs of your students. The essential elements of the Launch are:

- Ensuring students interact with the language of the problem several times
- Drawing on students' understanding of the context to make sense of the problem
- Considering the solution pathway they will start during Grapple Time

The ultimate goal of the Launch is to help students feel confident approaching and making sense of word problems. This step alone is a feat for many students. Relying on themselves (individually or as a class) to make sense of the problem without the teacher telling them exactly what to do and how to do it can be challenging at first. A daily practice of launching the problem will help students grow to trust themselves to take the steps to independently understand the problem.

Make the Launch routine fit your students' evolving needs. As students develop as problem solvers it is appropriate to remove scaffolds and ask students to give a problem a try with less launching support. Craft a Launch routine that takes into account your students' grade level, level of independence, and comfort with reading and making sense of word problems.

## A Launch Plan: Facilitating Problem Solving in the Launch

The purpose of the following five parts of the Launch is to help your students understand the problem. The key to success is knowing your students and tailoring the Launch to meet their specific needs. This five-part plan represents one common way the Launch is structured in Word Problem Workshop.

### Part 1: Tell the Story

Begin the Launch by telling the story of the problem. To pique students' interest and engage them in understanding the context of the story, you'll tell the story first instead of reading the problem word for word. Students' focus in this moment is not on solving or even remembering the numbers in the problem, but on understanding what is going on in the story.

Consider this word problem:

> *The baby shower needs enough tables and chairs for 52 people. The tables are round and seat 8 people. How many tables are needed for the baby shower?*

You might begin the Launch by telling the story of this problem like this:

"I was planning a baby shower for my brother and his wife. Have you ever been to a baby shower? Raise your hand if you have. A baby shower is a party to celebrate a new baby. Here is a picture from the baby shower. What do you notice? What do you wonder?

At the baby shower there are a lot of tables folded up in the corner of the room. My family and I have to set them up for the party. We have 52 people coming to the baby shower. So, we know we need enough chairs and tables for 52 people. Each table can fit 8 chairs around it. So before this party on Saturday I need to figure out how many tables we need to set up.

Do you think you can help me figure out how many tables we need so we can set up quickly on Saturday before the party?"

## Part 2: Embrace Expertise

Next we will work to embrace the expertise of each child. Really, we're doing this work throughout the Word Problem Workshop, but I've included it here as a step because this is an excellent time to elicit students' understanding and expertise around the context. Activating background knowledge connects what students know with their new learning. Often solving word problems is challenging because students don't fully read and think about the word problem in front of them. This step is an effort to connect students' current understanding to the problem, forging a personal connection and increasing their motivation to solve.

Sometimes you might solve a word problem that includes a context that is unfamiliar to some students. In this case, it is important to build students' understanding of the context of the word problem. This might include showing them a picture or asking a question of students to make connections between a new context and their background knowledge.

As you may have noticed in the baby shower example, these steps often meld together naturally. The teacher asked, "Have you been to a baby shower before? Here is a picture from the baby shower (Figure L.1) What do you notice? What do you wonder?"

**FIGURE L.1** A photo of the tables at my brother's baby shower that I used to launch the problem with students.

Now consider this word problem:

> *At the pumpkin patch there is a pumpkin house to take pictures with. Each shelf can hold 2 pumpkins. How many pumpkins are needed to fill the 4 walls of the house if each wall is a 4 by 6 array of shelves?*

Step 1: Launch

You might begin telling this story to students by saying, "Look at this picture (Figure L.2) of my family at a pumpkin patch. This is the pumpkin house. What do you notice? What do you wonder?"

Our students come to our classrooms with a wide range of experiences and it is vital to connect the "school math" contexts to their lives outside of school. Sometimes "school math" includes contexts that are unfamiliar to students, but with just a few moments of engaging in conversation with students about the new context, they can often make connections. At times this may mean building more background knowledge or spending a few minutes sharing different perspectives. I also find that by connecting problems to students' lives or my life we are able to build deeper connections to one another and mathematics. I look for ways to revise problems from the curriculum to include students, school events, or personal stories from my life.

**FIGURE L.2** A photo can help students understand an unfamiliar context, such as this pumpkin house, which they may not be familiar with.

## Part 3: Read and Retell

The strategies used in the Launch are designed to help students read and understand word problems. You'll notice many reading strategies embedded in the Launch routine, such as retelling, visualizing, and asking questions. The integration of reading skills is an intentional way to support all learners in accessing the context of the problem. By embedding the reading strategies within the Launch, we are able to support students' reading while also helping them focus on the math.

Next, you'll ask students to visualize the story by making a movie in their mind. You might say, "I'm going to read the problem again and this time I want you to see the problem in your mind. Make the pictures move when the problem has action. It will be like a movie in your mind. Ready?"

After this visualizing experience, it's time to engage students in retelling the problem to build and check their understanding. There are many ways to engage students with a retelling. A few options are:

- Choose two students to stand and retell the problem to the class.
- Ask students to do a quick turn-and-talk retelling with a partner.
- Tell students to do a whisper retell into their hands like they're telling a secret.

If you're doing a whole-class retelling, this is a great time to call on a student who needs a quick win to build confidence. Having their voice heard by the class and getting a celebratory cheer can really shift a child's mindset from "I can't do this" to "I think I'm ready to try."

Finding a retelling strategy that engages your students and gets them excited about understanding the problem is the key. You'll use your knowledge of your students to choose a retelling strategy that best fits your group on any given day.

The retell is also a good time to informally check for understanding so you know who may need support before Grapple Time. Look for engagement and evidence of understanding the problem. You'll use this information in Part 5 of the Launch, Just-Right Support.

## Part 4: Check for Understanding

We can use a single, brief question to assess students' understanding of the word problem during the Launch. This question will help gather information for supporting students during Grapple Time. Let's take a look at what asking this type of "more" or "fewer/less" question looks like in action. Consider this word problem:

*You have 32 dollars for the book fair. You spend 17 dollars on a book and a journal. How much money do you have left?*

You might ask the class, "After you go to the book fair, will you have more or less than 32 dollars?" Then, students will show either a signal for more (by putting their hands up next to their shoulders) or less (by moving their hands close together in front of their chest) (Figure L.3). Quickly glance around the room—students' responses may be an indicator of which students do not yet understand what the problem is asking them to figure out. You'll want to make a mental note to check in with them during the Grapple Time.

**FIGURE L.3** Student on the left is showing the "more" signal and the student on the right is showing the "less" signal.

Even when problems have different structures, we can often still ask a variation of the "more or less" question. For example, if the problem is:

*Josie has 4 brownies that she wants to share equally between 6 friends. How much brownie will each of the friends get?*

You might ask the class, "Will each person get more or less than $\frac{1}{2}$ of a brownie?"

Sometimes you will need to consider a benchmark to help students reason about the result. Using a benchmark like $\frac{1}{2}$ to help students reason about the brownie problem is more powerful than asking if each friend will get more or less than four brownies. Likely students have already figured out that this is an equal sharing problem and one child is not going to get all four brownies. However, pointing their attention to considering if each person will get more or less than $\frac{1}{2}$ of a brownie is helpful to both their solving and your assessment of their understanding. This, like all parts of Word Problem Workshop facilitation, will rely heavily on your knowledge of your students. You know your students best and are the expert on their strengths and growth areas. Trust yourself and trust the process. Give the "more or less" question a try and then make adjustments as you work through different problem types.

## Part 5: Give Just-Right Support

This last part of the Launch offers support for students who might need an extra moment before jumping into solving. Invite those students to stay with you briefly after the main part of the Launch for additional support. That invitation might sound like, "If you feel like you're ready to get started, head back to your tables. If you're not quite sure you understand the problem and want to talk about it more, stay at the carpet with me." Start by rereading the problem with these students and asking an open-ended question, such as, "Let's go back to the story. What do we know?" This question directs students' focus back to the problem details, reinforcing the importance of rereading and understanding the context of the problem, a skill we want them to become independent with over time. You could also help students break down the problem by asking, "What is the first thing you'll do to solve?" Once they have a plan for their first step, encourage them to start solving. Transition students into action without lingering too long so they gain confidence in moving forward with their own ideas.

I caution you to resist the urge to demonstrate strategies to students during this time, but instead focus on supporting students in making sense of the problem. When we see students struggle to understand a problem, it can be tempting to show or tell them what to do. Instead, remember that we are facilitating their thinking and understanding of the problem. Therefore, using questions that get students to examine the problem and come up with one idea for how to start is the goal of this quick huddle.

**Possible Ways to Provide Just-Right Support**

- Reread the problem together
- Ask students to identify the action in the problem
- Ask students to choose a first step for solving
- Give students a pep talk about mindset and strong mathematician behaviors

### In Action: The Launch

Let's take a look at what all the parts of the Launch look like in action with this problem:

> *There are 65 people waiting in line at the fair to ride the ferris wheel. Each gondola fits 5 people. How many gondolas will it take for all 65 people to get on the ferris wheel?*

**Part 1: Tell the Story**

"I was recently at the fair in my hometown in Michigan and the line for the ferris wheel was *really* long. There were sixty-five people waiting—I counted! I knew the wait was going to be long because each gondola only fits five people. My kids and I were wondering how many gondolas it would take to get all those people onto the ferris wheel."

**Part 2: Embrace Expertise**

The teacher asks students: "Have you ever visited a fair or been on a ferris wheel?" and "What do you notice about the ferris wheel in this picture?"

She points out the gondolas in the photo (Figure L.4). Some of the third graders may be unfamiliar with ferris wheels or use different words to describe where they sit on a ferris wheel. This visual will help students better understand the context and language of the problem in order to solve the word problem.

**Part 3: Read and Retell**

"Take a look at the problem up here on the board or on your paper—it's in both places. I'm going to read it while you follow along. I want you to make a movie in your mind. Close your eyes if you would like to, but really try to *see* the problem."

The teacher then reads the problem aloud to students and says, "Now, turn to your partner and retell the problem. Look back up here or at your paper if you forget the numbers."

**FIGURE L.4** A photo of a ferris wheel can help students understand a potentially unfamiliar term in the problem—gondola.

**Part 4: Check for Understanding**

"Will we need more or less than five gondolas to get the sixty-five people on the ride? Take a moment to think, and then show me a signal like this [shows an example of the more and less signal]. Will we need more [signal demonstration] or less [signal demonstration] to get the sixty-five people on the ride?"

**Part 5: Give Just-Right Support**

"I remember yesterday that some students had big feelings when they had to start over midway through solving. I want to remind you about our goal—*have the courage to try again when things go wrong*. We know that in problem solving we won't always get it right the first time, right? It really stinks to have to start again, but it takes a lot of courage to say you got it wrong and you have to try something else. Mathematicians often have to try again and again as they solve problems. I know you all can do this. I'm going to be looking around today to see examples of courage!"

"Max, Patrick, Marjorie and Stella, stay at the carpet, the rest of you head off to solve." Addressing just those four students once the others have left the carpet the teacher says, "Real quick I wanted to check to see how you're feeling about getting started solving—with your thumb showing me how ready you feel. Up—ready, middle—unsure, down—stuck." Students show their signals.

"Okay, I'm going to reread the problem. Then, I want you each to tell me what you might do first when you're back at your seat to solve. Okay?" The teacher reads the problem. "What will you do first, Max?"

"I'm going to get 65 cubes." Max replies.

"Okay, Stella?" the teacher asks.

Stella responds, "I'm going to do the same as Max then put them in groups of five." The other two students do the "same" signal.

"Alright, head off to your seats and solve. I can't wait to see what you come up with!" The teacher stands and gestures for the students to head back to their seats.

# Common Questions from Teachers

## What About the Students Who Can't Read Yet?

Each Launch layers in support for students with multiple read alouds of the problem, giving students the opportunity to follow along with the printed problem as you read a large version of the problem in the front of the class.

These resources support students in seeing the words and understanding the context. You can also change the language of word problems to make them more language accessible to your students.

The daily nature of the Launch as the first step of Word Problem Workshop helps students build the skills necessary to read, reread, retell, and ask questions about the word problem. Be explicit about naming the steps of the Launch as you move through them each day, as well as how students can use these with new problems they solve independently.

**FIGURE L.5** Mona listens in as kindergarten students get started working after the Launch.

For example, during a kindergarten Launch, many students could not yet read the problem on their own (Figure L.5). I pointed to the words as I read them aloud. Then I prompted the students to follow along as I read and try to find the word "crayons" in the problem. After they started the Grapple Time a student asked, "How many crayons?" I stopped the group and said, "Let's look back at the problem to remember how many crayons Jessie started with. Point if you see the number." Referring back to the problem helps students build the self-monitoring skills to check back to the problem, even if they can't read all the words yet.

## What if After the Launch Students Still Don't Get It?

Some students may not be ready to solve after the Launch. They may go into Grapple Time a bit lost and in need of more support. In the Grapple chapter we will discuss strategies students can use to get started. However, you may want to offer a bit more support during Part 5 (Just-Right Support) of the Launch. Encourage students to move into Grapple Time and try something to get started.

After you ask the check for understanding question you'll have a good idea of who might not understand what the problem is asking or might be headed off on the wrong foot down a solution pathway. These will be the students you go to first during Grapple Time. However, after the Launch, send students off to give it a try with confidence and enthusiasm. This opportunity to try something and grapple, even momentarily, is valuable for all students to experience.

### How Do I Launch the Five Word Problems That Are in My Students' Workbook?

I suggest you choose just one problem from the workbook to launch at first. This could be the task you feel is most worthy of discussing and unpacking. Not every problem needs to be launched. The goal is for students to experience the Launch and ultimately adopt the practices of reading and comprehending the problem when solving independently. In the Reflect step of Word Problem Workshop you can have students use what they learned to solve the remaining four problems in their workbook. As students make sense of these independent problems on their own, you can reinforce the strategies they are using to make sense of problems by noticing aloud what you see: "Nia is rereading the problem before she gets her cubes out," "I see Thomas started, and then went back to the problem to reread," "It looks like Selma isn't solving yet, but she's taking a second to get a movie in her mind."

## Be an Action Taker

### First Steps

- Try the first four steps of the Launch routine with a word problem from your curriculum.
- Find a photograph to display when launching a problem with an unfamiliar context.
- Teach students the signals for the Check for Understanding (Part 4 of the Launch) question. Practice using the more or less signals.

## Ready to Run

- Plan to do the Word Problem Workshop Launch routine daily for a week, then reflect on how many students were prepared to grapple after the Launch.
- Add in Part 5 of the Launch to support students who might be struggling to understand the problem and are not quite ready to grapple.
- Revise the Launch routine to fit the needs of your students.

# Step 2: Grapple

The radar crept forward, displaying a kaleidoscope of rain and storms headed directly for the twenty tents my third graders had proudly popped earlier that day. Just an hour ago, the excited campers had finally quieted down and fallen asleep. Now I lay in my one-person tent, eyes glued to my phone's dwindling battery and the weather app, debating whether to evacuate our students into the small kitchen on the farm grounds where we were camping.

"Mona!! Did you look at the weather?" a loud whisper came from beyond the zipper of my tent. It was Lauren—she was thinking exactly what I was. Slipping on my shoes, I met her outside and said, "We've got to get them out of the tents, don't we?!" We had approximately fifteen minutes to move forty-six sleeping kids before the storm hit.

At 11:57 pm we began rousing the campers with gentle but urgent whispers: "Get your shoes on, grab your sleeping bag, and walk to the kitchen. Quickly!" Kids stirred—scared, frazzled, and some frozen in place. But it was in this chaotic moment that I saw the fruits of our Grapple Time shine through.

The students took action in the face of uncertainty, supported one another, and didn't leave anyone behind. I heard words we'd practiced daily during Grapple Time: "We can do hard things." "We just have to try our best right now." "Let me help you." They weren't all calm, but they were all patient and helpful, facing the challenge with confidence and in community.

By 12:15 am the last camper laid their sleeping bag down on the few remaining inches of the kitchen floor as the rain started to pour. Whispers filled the room: "Whoa, that was crazy. We're like real explorers!" "We did it—we got out together." "I think that was real grappling, Ms. Iehl!" Lauren and I sat on the kitchen counter, listening to the rain pound down and watching the lightning flash outside. We looked out at the floor crowded with not just sleeping kids, but real-life problem solvers. Beaming with pride, we reflected on how well the kids handled the unexpected, and it gave us a glimpse into the true impact of Grapple Time.

The storm was gone by the morning, leaving behind a fallen tree branch on a tent. Despite the chaos it caused the night before, the storm revealed something remarkable: a group of third graders facing a storm together with confidence, patience, and teamwork. This transformation wasn't just luck—it was the result of creating a culture in which struggle isn't something to fear but rather to embrace. Like that stormy night, it's the combination of challenge and support that empowers students to believe, "We've got this!" even when the stakes are high and the obstacles feel insurmountable.

## Grappling is a Pathway to Sense-Making

Though math class doesn't involve storms and tents, it mirrors that stormy night in its demands for persistence, effort, and teamwork in the face of challenges. Students enter Grapple Time expecting to tackle a tough problem that might feel overwhelming at first. Like those campers in the storm, they encourage one another and courageously try to make sense of the math and find solutions. All the while, the teacher is there facilitating and ensuring everyone keeps moving along the problem-solving path. When the struggle clears, students emerge more confident and knowledgeable, having faced the challenge and used it as a stepping stone to deeper understanding and growth.

Years ago, I had a third-grade student named Kevonte. Grapple Time, the heart of our Word Problem Workshop, was a challenge for him. "I'm not gonna do this," he'd declare, shutting down before even starting. Beneath his defiance was fear—fear of making mistakes and looking "stupid" in front of his classmates. As I got to know Kevonte better, I learned that he worried about seeming weak, and when those big feelings bubbled over, they often came out as outbursts, both verbal and physical.

We worked every day to build his confidence and help him develop strategies for making sense of problems. Grapple Time still wasn't always easy for Kevonte, and challenges often pushed him to his limits. But little by little, he started to take risks. He learned to make sense of problems without shutting down. He discovered that his ideas had value, even if they weren't perfect. Kevonte began participating in our discussions, offering his strategies, and staying engaged—though not without the occasional tough day.

Two years later, I taught Kevonte again in fifth grade and I saw how far he'd come. One day during Grapple Time, he was tipping in his chair and chatting with a classmate. "Kevonte, it's Grapple Time. Get to work," I said. He smirked, adjusted his chair, grabbed his pencil, and said, "Yep. Got it, Ms. Iehl."

After class, he stopped me. "I could've never done that in third grade," he said. Thinking he meant the fraction problem, I started to respond, but he clarified: "No, I mean getting back to work after you called me out. That used to make me so upset I couldn't even think about math. I was scared of what people thought of me. Now I know—it's fine. Everyone makes mistakes. Just fix it and keep going."

In that moment, I saw how Grapple Time had prepared Kevonte to weather storms, not just in math but in life.

> **We can** support students in developing perseverance and the mindset to see mistakes as opportunities for learning by grappling with word problems daily. Grappling strengthens problem-solving skills, deepens mathematical understanding, and empowers students to tackle complex problems confidently.

## Grappling Grows Mathematicians

After your class has read and made sense of the word problem (Step 1: Launch), it is time for Step 2 of Word Problem Workshop—Grapple Time. Grapple Time is an independent student work time in which productive struggle is expected and celebrated. During this time students try different strategies, take risks (possibly making mistakes along the way), work through road blocks, and build understanding over time.

Struggling with problems, taking risks, and making mistakes during Grapple Time does not always feel natural or comfortable for many students (or adults!). In fact, in my experience many students resist struggling at first. As Tracy Zager writes in *Becoming the Math Teacher You Wish You'd Had*, grappling with problems often "involves attempting some mathematics without being certain of the outcome. It might involve asking a question, taking a stab at a different strategy, working with unfamiliar numbers or operations, looking for a relationship, or imagining an alternate scenario" (2017, 50). In our classrooms we can prepare our students to take mathematical risks through the ways we structure and facilitate Grapple Time.

This chapter focuses on using Grapple Time to support students' growth as mathematicians. In the first part of the chapter, we'll look at how to prepare ourselves and students for Grapple Time. In the second part of the chapter, we explore how to support students as problem solvers specifically during Grapple Time (Step 2 of Word Problem Workshop).

### Goals of Grapple Time

- Develop a mindset that embraces challenge and sees mistakes as learning opportunities
- Take risks to uncover new understandings
- Clearly show reasoning and problem-solving steps on paper
- Engage with the teacher during one-on-one conferences to deepen understanding

## Part 1: Preparing for Grapple Time

### *Lean in to Productive Struggle*

Grapple Time can be a powerful tool for fostering student growth, but without the right preparation, it can quickly turn into a source of frustration. Many teachers, excited to dive in, jump straight into Grapple Time without setting the stage. The result? Students in tears, confusion, and even angry emails from parents. To avoid this, we must first create a safe and welcoming math community that supports students' risk-taking and ensures they understand the process of grappling before we begin.

Understanding when struggle is productive and when it is just a downward spiral toward overwhelm is a good place to start. Consider the characteristics of productive and unproductive struggle noted in Figure G.1. When students are engaged in productive struggle they have some ideas to try out, they make progress, and they can discuss their ideas. When struggle has become unproductive a student may not know where to begin, may feel defeated or may not have made any forward progress in quite some time. Understanding the difference between productive and unproductive struggle can help us know when a student might just need more time or gentle support and when we may need to rethink the task or our approach.

**Unproductive Struggle**
- No progress
- Disengaged
- Limited understanding
- Learning goal unclear
- Feels confused, frustrated, stuck

**Productive Struggle**
- Actively engaged
- Flexible thinking
- Leads to understanding
- Learning goal clear
- Feels empowered, confident, and supported

**FIGURE G.1** Knowing the characteristics of productive and unproductive struggle can help teachers facilitate Grapple Time.

## Reframe Mistakes as Stepping Stones

Grapple Time is our opportunity to help students embrace mistakes as part of learning, to shift their focus from simply finding the right answer to finding the joy in discovering, sense-making, and exploring the problem.

Low-stakes mistakes during Grapple Time build the resilience and decision-making skills our students will need for bigger challenges they will inevitably face later in math and in life. Tinkering and trying out new ideas to see what works and what doesn't are fundamentally important processes in mathematics (and many kinds of learning!). By framing errors as acts of courage and curiosity, we can create classroom communities in which students feel safe taking risks, embracing struggle, and learning to persist through challenges.

Ultimately, Grapple Time is about much more than solving word problems—it's about creating confident, resilient learners who see mistakes as stepping stones to growth. It's about fostering a mindset where exploration, critical thinking, and ownership of their learning are at the core. Grappling allows students to find fulfillment in exploring and making sense of a problem. In the end, they experience the satisfaction that comes from working through a challenge to discover a solution.

This shift won't happen overnight, and that's okay. Give both yourself and your students the time and space to grow. With consistent practice, you'll start to see the change. In just a few weeks, your students will begin using the language around Grapple Time you've modeled, approaching challenges with persistence instead of frustration, and embracing the process of grappling with confidence. This is the power of Grapple Time.

## Set Expectations for Grapple Time

Grapple Time may feel like a different way of learning for many students (and teachers!). It should be a time for students to be creative, take risks, and find comfort in knowing that there will be support along the way. Grapple Time is an opportunity for students to give new ideas and solution pathways a try. However, in order to do this work there must be very clear expectations so that the routine of Grapple Time feels predictable and the time is productive.

It is important to have explicit conversations about what it means to learn math and the role that struggle plays during Grapple Time. Build on the math norms you co-created with students, and hone in on what it will look like, sound like, and feel like to grapple. One way to lead this conversation is by making connections to times when students learned something else new. Ask students to reflect on when they learned to ride a bike, swim, read, tie their shoes, or play a game. Likely in all of these instances students experienced some struggle and had to grapple in order to improve. Ask students to reflect on:

- What did it take to get better?
- What did it look like / sound like / feel like when you were struggling to ____?
- What helped you improve?
- What about when we are struggling with a word problem? (Repeat the same questions as above!)

In Figure G.2 are examples of anchor charts that can serve as references during Grapple Time. These charts often have reminders of what students should do during Grapple Time, but also normalize the feelings that come along with struggle.

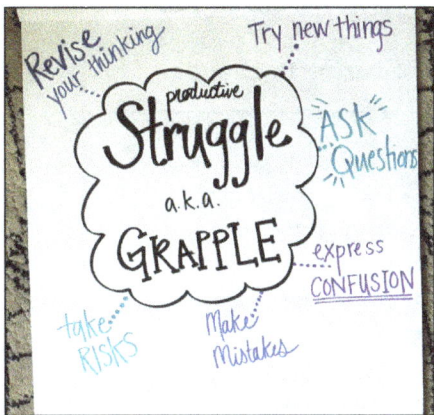 
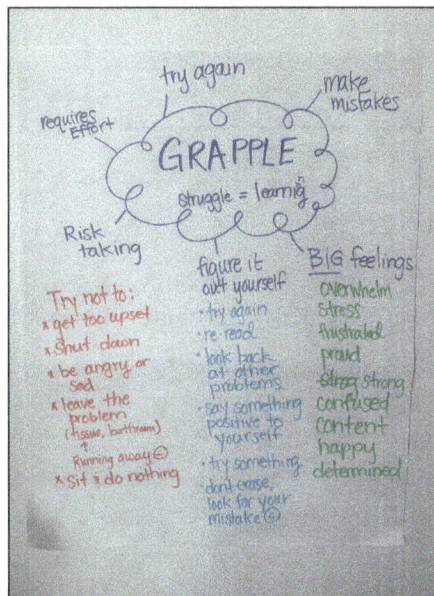 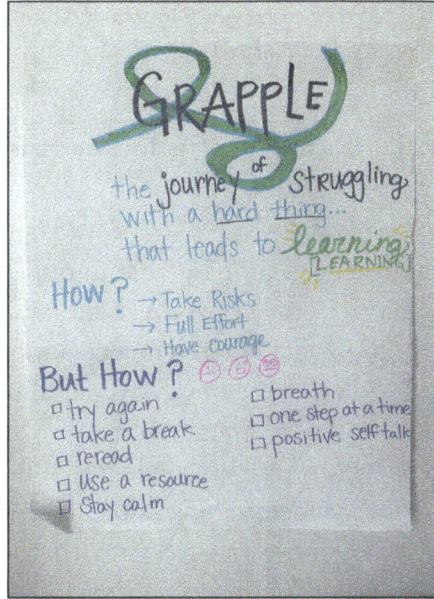

**FIGURE G.2** Grapple Time anchor charts from four classrooms.

## Define Student and Teacher Roles During Grapple Time

With an understanding of the goals of Grapple Time, now we can focus on the roles that both the teacher and students take on during this part of Word Problem Workshop (Figure G.3). Building on the trust and relationships we've cultivated, these roles are crucial to making Grapple Time effective and engaging for every student.

*Step 2: Grapple* **63**

| Teachers are... | Students are... |
|---|---|
| • Setting clear expectations<br>• Providing time and space for productive struggle<br>• Observing & taking notes<br>• Maintaining a neutral stance<br>• Asking open-ended questions<br>• Offering subtle guidance through "nuggets and nudges" | • Attempting to solve<br>• Facing challenges, getting stuck and experiencing both frustration and joy<br>• Trying new approaches<br>• Applying prior knowledge<br>• Showing their thinking |

**FIGURE G.3** The roles of teachers and students during Grapple Time.

### The Teacher's Role During Grapple Time

The teacher's primary role during Grapple Time is to create a space for students to problem solve and experience productive struggle. Resist the urge to explicitly teach students a procedure or "show them what to do." Instead, encourage exploration, allowing students to use what they know to solve the problem. After a few minutes of getting started with Grapple Time, conference with students and offer nudges or nuggets of information to move students along in their solving and understanding.

At times we may feel tempted to step in and rescue students when we see them making mistakes. In *Principles to Actions: Ensuring Mathematical Success for All*, the National Council of Teachers of Mathematics (NCTM) asserts:

> *Teachers sometimes perceive student frustration or lack of immediate success as indicators that they have somehow failed their students. As a result, they jump in to "rescue" students by breaking down the task and guiding students step by step through the difficulties. Although well intentioned, such "rescuing" undermines the efforts of students, lowers the cognitive demand of the task, and deprives students of opportunities to engage fully in making sense of mathematics.*
>
> (2014, 48)

NCTM's message underscores the importance of how we respond to students' mistakes. Rescuing students sends the message that we don't believe they can succeed without the teacher's help every step of the way. Instead, we must trust in their ability to work through challenges. Our role is not to prevent struggle, but to support students as they navigate their own solution pathways. Giving students some space to work through challenges may feel uncomfortable at times, but it is essential for helping students develop the confidence and skills to solve problems on their own. We are there to offer gentle guidance, but the thinking and problem solving must come from them.

### The Students' Role During Grapple Time

During Grapple Time, students must take ownership of solving the problem. They will need to think critically, make mathematical decisions, and apply what they know. Sometimes, this means students might use strategies that aren't "on grade level" or methods you didn't explicitly teach the day before. This part of Word Problem Workshop is about letting students have a go at the problem using what they know. Then, during the next parts of Word Problem Workshop, students will build on their understandings. First though, students must have the experience of making sense of the problem and trying out a strategy for solving.

As students dive into the problem, look for students who are:

- Using a strategy they can explain
- Using manipulatives or models to make sense of the problem
- Able to explain their choices
- Talking about the numbers in the problem within the context of the problem

These behaviors are the foundation of independent problem solving and are key to students' mathematical growth in Grapple Time. Just as we make the behavior expectations clear during Word Problem Workshop and support them with lessons and norms, we also need to do the same for the mathematical problem-solving behaviors.

## *Encourage Students to Show Their Math Thinking During Grapple Time*

How many times have you asked your students to show their work, only to be met with blank stares and blank papers? Until we start showing kids *why* showing their work is important, they won't do it. We can all agree that showing math thinking is an essential mathematical behavior.

It is also an important math norm because showing their thinking on paper during Grapple Time allows students to share and communicate with the mathematical community in the next parts of Word Problem Workshop. So, in order to get students to show their reasoning and justify their answers with clear models and strategies we have to be clear about what we expect. Then, give students time to practice and reflect on their progress.

"I can show my math thinking" is a learning goal students can work on from kindergarten all the way through elementary school (and beyond). Students will work toward this learning goal in developmentally appropriate ways according to their age and grade. I encourage individual grade-level teams to come together and discuss what this looks like for their students. In Figure G.4 you'll see two examples of anchor charts that support students to clearly communicate their math thinking.

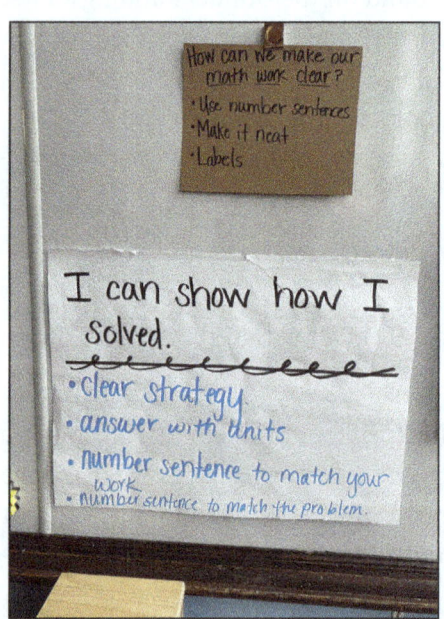 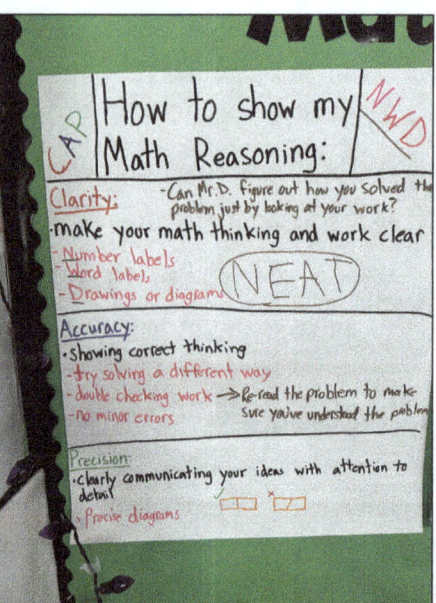

**FIGURE G.4** Examples of two different anchor charts to encourage students to show their thinking on paper.

To help students express their thinking more clearly, consider providing a criteria list for what it means to "show or explain your reasoning" using three categories: clarity, accuracy, and precision. Below in Figure G.5 you will find a sample criteria list you can adapt for your grade level.

### Make Your Math Thinking
**Clear**
**Accurate**
**Precise**

| Clear | Accurate | Precise |
|---|---|---|
| • Organized<br>• Easy to understand | • Correct<br>• Minor errors are fixed<br>• Answers the question completely (all parts) | • Attention to detail<br>• Representations are (reasonably) exact<br>• Consistent |
| **How?**<br>• Use labels and units<br>• Explain in words, numbers or symbols how you know / how you solved<br>• Use reasonably neat handwriting<br>• Remove unnecessary information or "extras" | **How?**<br>• Check your work<br>• Use another strategy<br>• Double check that you copied the formula, numbers, etc. correctly from the problem<br>• Reread the problem<br>• Write an equation to represent the situation (problem) | **How?**<br>• Models are representative of the quantities (proportional)<br>• Fractions are represented as equal parts<br>• Number lines are partitioned with reasonable precision<br>**Examples:**<br>THIS: (number line from 18, 20 with +2, to 77 with +57)<br>NOT THIS: (number line 18, 20, 77 with +2 and +57 equally spaced)<br>THIS: Tens Ones (2 tens rods, 8 ones cubes)<br>NOT THIS: Ones Tens (3 large squares labeled Ones, 2 small lines labeled Tens) |

**FIGURE G.5** This criteria list can be adapted for your grade level to support the learning goal "I can show my math thinking clearly, accurately, and precisely."

## Clarity

Clarity is how clear and understandable your work is to others. That means someone could look at your math work on paper or with manipulatives and see clearly what you did. For our students, this means their reasoning is organized and easy to understand. One way this clarity can be achieved is through adding labels to their work. For example, if the problem is about rows of chairs in the gym for the band concert, students might label "rows" and "chairs" with words, and perhaps also label the number of chairs in each row and the rows themselves. Labeling their answer with units is another way students can make their work clear.

## Accuracy

Being accurate means achieving the goal. This means students' reasoning and strategies make sense for the problem. Students avoid minor errors by checking their work with multiple strategies and double checking that they did not make any small calculation errors. The answer should be a complete response to the question that is asked in the problem and no parts are missed. Accuracy is often achieved when students reread the problem and use multiple strategies to check their work to ensure it is complete and correct.

## Precision

Precision is mathematical consistency, attention to detail, and reliability. Precision means students draw mathematical models proportionally and with care to ensure they represent the quantities accurately. For example, when showing a rectangle partitioned into fourths, each part is equal, or when representing a number using drawings of base-ten blocks, the tens and ones should appear different and proportional.

# Part 2: Facilitating Productive Struggle During Grapple Time

The teacher's role during Word Problem Workshop is to be a facilitator of math thinking and the students' role is to be the thinkers and doers of math. During Grapple Time we want students to be doing the math and that means our job as the facilitator is to ensure students are staying in productive struggle space without becoming overly frustrated.

## Staying Neutral to Get Curious

It is natural to want to jump in and support students, especially when they are struggling. However, resisting this urge during Grapple Time is one of the greatest gifts we can give our students. By being less helpful, we allow students the space to think, make decisions, and solve independently.

Take a neutral stance by observing students work. Don't judge or intervene too quickly. Instead, ask open-ended questions that get students to articulate their thinking. Listen carefully, with a genuine interest in understanding your students' thinking. Get curious about their strategies. I often say I am "mining for the gems in their thinking!" These gems might be their unique strategies, mathematical insights, or areas of confusion. By taking this stance of being curious about students' thinking we can truly begin to understand students' perspectives and what they are able to do independently.

Staying neutral does not mean abandoning students entirely. There are certainly times for teacher questioning, nudges, and even explicit teaching; however, giving students the time and space to "have a go" with a problem first encourages independence, strengthens their confidence, and shows them they are capable.

That said, be cautious not to shift your focus from promoting sense-making and reasoning to managing student behavior, fixing errors, or ensuring students finish the task. While we may need to address behavior or nudge students to keep working, the priority is on understanding students' thinking.

### In Action: Staying Neutral During Grapple Time

Just as students sit down to begin to grapple, a student raises their hand, seeking help before attempting to solve. Ms. Brady knows this student well and is confident they have what they need to get started. So she signals for the student to put his hand down and keep going, pointing to the Grapple Time anchor chart on the wall. The student keeps their hand up, with a grimace on their face and a dramatic shrug-sigh. A few more seconds go by, and after the student takes a visible deep breath, he picks up the pencil and starts writing something on his paper. After several minutes, Ms. Brady makes her way to the student and says, "How's it going?"

> **SECOND-GRADE STUDENT:** (Pointing at their paper) I need help. Ugh, is this even right?
> **MS. BRADY:** Hmm… you need help? Tell me what you're thinking.

STUDENT: Ummm... I just started to do something, anything. I just... ugh. I don't know what to do—is it right?

Ms. BRADY: Tell me more about what you were thinking here. (Points at the student's strategy written on the paper)

STUDENT: I started at 159 people at the baseball game and added the people that came on the number line with these jumps until I got to the 318 total people at the game.

Ms. BRADY: Okay. Is there another way you can try to solve to confirm your answer? Give it a try, I'll be back.

The teacher walks away as the student looks back at the problem and starts to draw base-ten blocks on their paper.

This interaction demonstrates how a teacher can support the student who is developing confidence in their mathematical ability, not by taking away their agency and becoming the expert, but by supporting the student to stay in control of their reasoning and math thinking. Before Ms. Brady offered any math advice, she refocused students on the Grapple Chart. She also used her deep knowledge of her students to decide what level of support to give; in this case, she knew this student mostly needed encouragement to dig into the math and check their ideas with multiple strategies. You might also notice that the teacher only asked questions ("You need help?" "Can you tell me what you're thinking?" "Can you tell me more about your thinking here?" "Is there another way you can solve to confirm your answer?") This is an intentional move. Ms. Brady tries to communicate confidence in the students' ability and nudges them to not rely on her for reasoning, but instead she is a neutral sounding board. By staying neutral, we show respect for students' ideas and expertise, creating space for them to showcase what they know and can do.

Staying neutral often means:

- Maintaining a neutral facial expression and body language
- Assuming a listening stance so that the students can clearly explain their thinking
- Using questions to find out more about students' thinking
- Offering students a possible option for an action step to take next ("Is there another way you can confirm your answer?"), while communicating that the choice is theirs

## Support Struggle

A neutral stance isn't the only way we facilitate a successful Grapple Time. We also must be in tune with our students, recognizing when they are truly stuck or in need of support. There is a difference between a student who is eliciting our approval or working through a moment of uncertainty and one who is defeated or truly stuck. Our goal is to find these students just in the nick of time to offer the support that will keep them moving forward—before they completely shut down.

Juli Dixon, Lisa A. Brooks, and Melissa R. Carli, authors of *Making Sense of Mathematics for Teaching the Small Group*, write about the difference between "just in case" and "just in time" scaffolds (Dixon et al. 2018). "Just in case" scaffolds preemptively offer explanations or hints before students show the need for support. While well intentioned, this approach robs students of the opportunity to explore and problem solve the challenging task. In fact, this type of "pre-teaching" actually prevents students from engaging in productive struggle. "Just in case" scaffolding can train students to wait for the teacher to tell them what to do instead of building their problem-solving independence.

In contrast, "just in time" scaffolds provide support only when struggle becomes unproductive—when students encounter a genuine roadblock (Dixon et al. 2018). These scaffolds enable students to continue their problem-solving journey without taking away their agency. By addressing misconceptions in the moment, we ensure all students can access the task equitably, avoiding labels that suggest they can't succeed without intervention. These "just in time" supports may come in the form of one-on-one conferences, small-group work, or future follow-up lessons.

## Nudge or a Nugget

So what does this "just in time" kind of support look like in Word Problem Workshop? And how can we support students in ways that don't take away their agency or confidence? Whether students are stuck on making sense of the problem, unpacking unknown vocabulary, or choosing a first step to take to solve the problem, giving just a small moment of support is often enough to get kids back on the problem-solving pathway. This is where the concept of a nudge or nugget (Figure G.6) comes in. During Grapple Time, we can support students with targeted questions and small pieces of information that help them move forward without solving the problem for them.

**Nudge:**
- I notice...
- How can you?
- What will you do next?
- Have you done something like this before?
- How could you show your thinking on paper?
- What does the problem say?

**Nugget:**
- When you draw your fraction model, remember equal parts.
- I see you have a number line, can you use that to help add up?
- You can break up a number into tens and ones. Will that help?
- Look back at the chart from yesterday, see how Jamal solved. What do you notice?

**FIGURE G.6** Nudges are questions with the purpose of sparking a new thought within the student. A nugget is a tiny piece of mathematical information that students may need to continue.

## What's a Nudge?

A nudge is a strategic question or prompt that gets the student thinking about the problem context, their representation, or their math reasoning. Its purpose is to help students re-engage with their thinking and take the next step in solving the problem. Remember, during Grapple Time, we are empowering students to solve and develop their understanding through experience. However, students sometimes need a small push to get started or continue working. Even as adults, we rely on thought partners to stay on track—students are no different.

A nudge might take the form of a question like:

- What do you notice in the problem?
- What does this number represent?
- How could you show this in a different way?

These questions are quick and focused on shifting students' attention or encouraging them to revisit their thinking.

Nudges are for all students, not just those struggling. The nudge is brief and intentional—offering just enough support to help students move forward without dictating the next step.

### In Action: A Nudge

One afternoon, a few years ago, I was teaching in a first-grade classroom. The students were solving this problem:

*There are 14 students sitting on the carpet in Ms. Ryan's room. 6 students left the carpet. How many students are sitting on the carpet now?"*

As I observed students getting started on this problem, I saw one student place fourteen blocks in front of him, enthusiastically counting them by twos several times. After watching him for a few moments, I said, "Counting by twos is really cool! I wonder, will counting by twos help you find out how many kids are sitting on the carpet now?"

The student just briefly looked up, smiled, and went right back to counting by twos. I decided to try again. "You're really good at counting by twos! Where are the kids on the carpet?" This time, he stopped and put his hands flat on the table, signaling to me that I was interrupting him. "I'm going to count by twos."

"Okay," I responded. "I can't wait to see how it goes. Maybe you'll be able to figure out how many students are at the carpet now." Students don't always accept a nudge. In this case, I tried to nudge the first grader toward engaging with the question in the problem, but ultimately, he chose to stay on his path. And that's okay—it's his solution journey and he will have many opportunities to engage with the problem on this day and other problems on subsequent days.

Here's the thing about supporting students' thinking: we can offer ideas, but we can't force kids to think or do. Maybe it's not the right time for him to make the connection, or maybe my nudge didn't resonate with him yet. Or perhaps he was just excited about his newfound ability to count by twos and wanted to practice that skill. In time, with more exploration and discussion, this student's understanding will evolve. That's the trust we have in our students: they are the problem solvers and we are here to facilitate thinking. In the end, though, it is their thinking that drives the learning.

## What's a Nugget?

Like the nudge, a nugget is a small, purposeful prompt designed to support a student's thinking. A nugget offers just enough information to help students see a connection, clarify a concept, or refine their strategy. We can think about nuggets in a few different categories.

**Nuggets that support students getting started or navigating a sticky spot might include:**

- Pointing out a connection to a previously discussed math concept ("What you're trying here reminds me of the strategy Jacobi shared yesterday.")

- Directing students to an anchor chart or previous student work. ("You can take a look at the chart on the wall with Jacobi's strategy from yesterday." "Which of these strategies we talked about yesterday would you like to try today?")

- Collaboratively starting or completing a small task, like counting manipulatives together. ("You said that when the word problem starts, Grandpa has fifteen cookies. Could we show what that would look like with these cubes?")

- Identifying patterns or mistakes in their reasoning to spur a second look. ("I see you have twenty cookies on your paper. Can you point to where in the story told you there were twenty cookies?")

**Nuggets that deepen understanding of math concepts might include:**

- Helping students reason about base-ten relationships (making a ten, regrouping, breaking down a hundred into ten tens, etc.) ("We've been talking about making a ten. Can that help you here?")

- Supporting students in creating equal groups to represent division or multiplication ("What does the problem say about how many are in each group?")

- Encouraging reasoning about a remainder within the context of a problem ("What will you do with this leftover three pieces of candy?" "How will these seven remaining students go to the field trip if the buses are full?")

- Breaking numbers apart (decomposing) to make computation easier ("Can you break these numbers down to be more efficient?")

- Highlighting relationships between addition and subtraction or multiplication and division ("I see you are subtracting. Can you show me what in the story told you to subtract?")

**Nuggets that support strategy use and decision making might include:**

- Asking, "Will this strategy help you get an answer?" or "Does this strategy always work?"

- Suggesting adding up in "chunks" to find the answer to a subtraction problem ("That's a lot of minus ten, minus ten, minus ten, and so on. I wonder if there is a faster way to subtract those tens?")

- Showing how decomposing a number can be represented using base-ten blocks ("You built eighty-seven with the base-ten blocks. Where are the tens? Ones? What is the value of these eight sticks? How do you know for sure?")

- Encouraging students to reflect on the question, "What makes your strategy efficient or effective?"

## When Should You Offer a Nudge or Nugget?

Before offering a nudge or nugget, it is important to first take time to understand the student's thinking. Listen carefully to the student's thinking and observe their work. Get curious about their approach and perspective. What are they doing that makes sense? What might be the next step? Once you think you understand their thinking, check in with the student by summarizing what they have told or shown you. For example, this might sound like, "So, you're using base-ten blocks to represent the two numbers in the problem. Let's look at how you grouped them—what do you notice about the tens and ones?"

In the next section we will discuss how you'll choose who to conference with and support during Grapple Time. You'll offer nuggets and nudges during Move 1: Scan and Move 4: Ask.

# Four Moves to Facilitating Thinking During Grapple Time

As the facilitator, your role is to spark students' thinking and leverage their ideas to inspire deeper mathematical reasoning among the entire class. Let's take a look at four moves (Figure G.7) you can use during Grapple Time to support productive struggle, nurture students' problem solving and lay the groundwork for a meaningful math discussion.

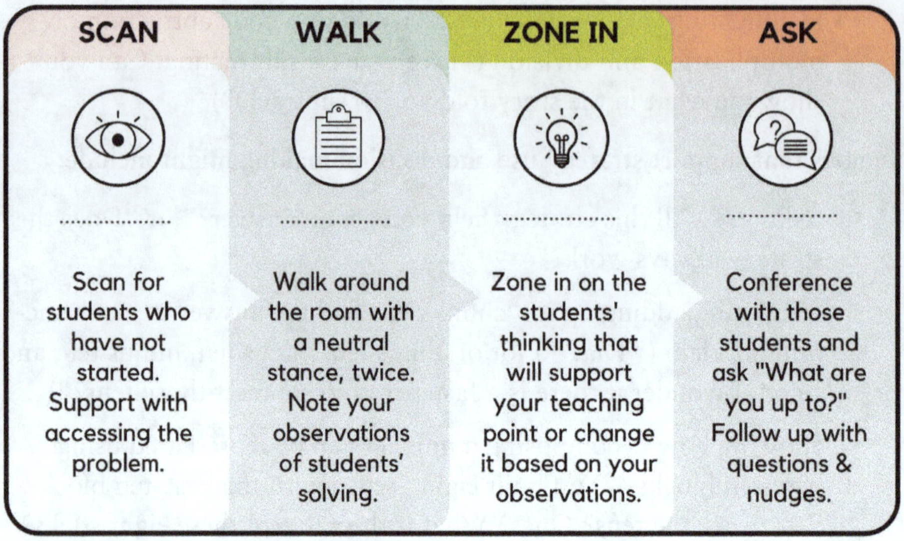

| SCAN | WALK | ZONE IN | ASK |
|---|---|---|---|
| Scan for students who have not started. Support with accessing the problem. | Walk around the room with a neutral stance, twice. Note your observations of students' solving. | Zone in on the students' thinking that will support your teaching point or change it based on your observations. | Conference with those students and ask "What are you up to?" Follow up with questions & nudges. |

**FIGURE G.7** Four teacher moves for Grapple Time.

## Move 1: Scan

Within the first few minutes of Grapple Time, scan the classroom to get a sense of where everyone is in getting started with solving. Pay attention to students who have momentarily paused or are showing signs of frustration. I recommend scanning the room multiple times during this initial phase of Grapple Time. Think of yourself as the lifeguard at the busy summer pool. You'll be watching for students who are confidently engaged, those on the verge of struggling, and those who are in need of immediate help. Your priority will be the students who need the most support. These may be students you've identified during the check for understanding question at the end of the Launch.

As you scan, consider:

- Are students making progress, or do they seem stuck?
- Who might need support to get started?
- Are any students showing signs of frustration or confusion who need immediate attention?

Once you've identified students who need immediate support, go to those students to get started with a quick nudge or a nugget.

## Move 2: Walk

After ensuring the class is off to a good start, take a few moments to walk around the room and observe. This is your time to notice patterns in how students are solving the problem. By giving yourself the space to simply observe, you'll begin to see where the class is in their thinking.

As you walk, you may notice that some students are experiencing the same misconception or that many students are using a similar strategy. You could even be surprised by students who are using strategies you hadn't anticipated. This walk allows you, as the facilitator, to get a sense of what's happening in the room before zoning in on specific students who may need more focused support.

During this time, take note of students' strategies. You might use a simple recording (Figure G.8) sheet where you can quickly jot down how each student is solving. As you walk around the classroom, consider:

- Are most students solving the problem with a similar strategy, or is there a wide range of different strategies?

- Are students' approaches to the problem helping them engage with the learning goal?

- Does what you see match what you anticipated students would do?

- Is there a pattern (misconception, common strategy, or a fixable mistake) that stands out?

Once you've gathered some general insight, you'll start focusing on conferring with a few students (Move 3). The insights you've gathered on your walk will equip you to focus on helping students move forward in their thinking during these conferences.

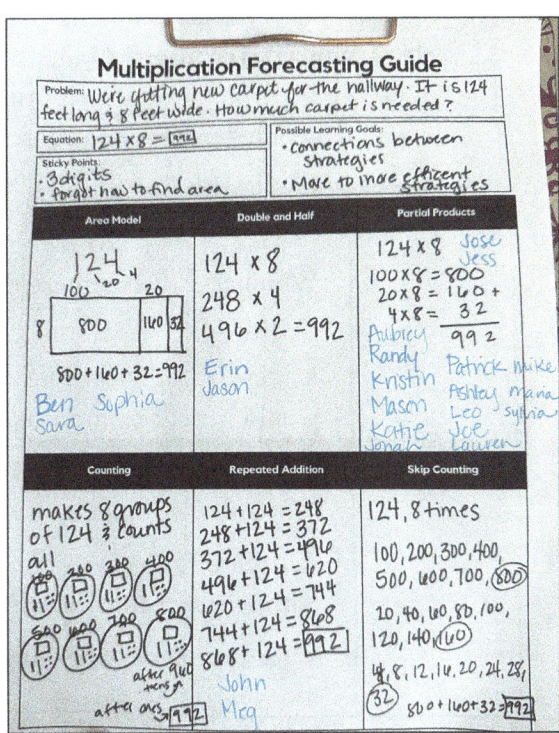

**FIGURE G.8** A Forecasting Guide is created during planning and used during Grapple Time to keep track of students' strategies and models. For more on Forecasting Guides, see the Planning for Word Problem Workshop chapter.

## Move 3: Zone In

Now that your students are solving and you've taken a few moments to walk around the room and observe them, it's time to zone in for a closer look. "Zoning in," in this context, means choosing a few students whose ideas and thinking you want to learn more about on that day.

*Step 2: Grapple* **77**

Consider the learning goal you planned for this Word Problem Workshop and the ways students are engaging with this goal. Think about how the learning goal aligns with what students are currently doing and which strategies or misconceptions stand out as opportunities to move the class forward. You'll want to take these ideas into account as you choose students to zone in on. This is the time to identify which students' thinking you might highlight in the discussion following Grapple Time in order to help the rest of the class make progress toward the goal.

Zoning in has two main purposes: 1) to investigate which students' strategies or reasoning you might highlight in the whole-group discussion, and 2) to decide who you will offer nudges and nuggets that support and deepen individual students' thinking.

While it is natural to want to conference with every student during Grapple Time, it is important to prioritize quality over quantity. Even though you may only have time to confer with a handful of students each day, over time, you will confer with every student multiple times.

As you select the students you'll confer with on any given day, consider:

- Who has a clear representation or strategy that could serve as an example for others?

- Is there a student whose representation or strategy most of the class would benefit from seeing or discussing?

- Is there a unique or more advanced approach that could spark curiosity or new thinking?

- Are there students using a more sophisticated strategy that aligns with where the majority of the class is headed?

- Which students' work aligns closely with the learning goal for today?

- Are there two strategies that we might compare in order to more deeply understand the mathematics?

Many times, you'll find multiple examples of students' work to highlight. You'll see a lot of strong math thinking and many different strategies or examples that *could* be shared with the class. As you observe and confer with students you'll gain more information that will help you make the decision. Your expertise in the math content and as the facilitator will guide you in selecting students whose ideas will move the whole class forward. In the Planning for Word Problem Workshop chapter, we will plan for these decisions using a simple framework that you can adopt to simplify your planning practice.

### *Move 4: Ask*

As you begin to notice patterns in how students are solving the problem and identify a few students whose thinking you want to know more about in this particular moment, it's time to talk to them. There are many reasons why students might be doing what they are doing, and we won't know the important details of students' thinking unless we ask them. This is the time we will ask students about their thinking and math work. You might start the conversation with "How's it going?" or "What are you up to?" These opening questions serve as an invitation to students to describe what they are doing (or not doing, if they're stuck) and share their thinking.

Once students have described their thinking, you'll quickly assess what's going on and choose a next step. That might mean you offer a nudge or a nugget. As you may recall from earlier in the chapter, both a nudge and a nugget are ways to provide support without taking away a student's opportunity to problem solve. We want students to continue to problem solve and reason about the mathematics. This is not the time to take their pencil and show them what to do. Instead, our teacher moves in this moment should serve to give students just enough to help them keep going and to reinvigorate their excitement for solving.

### Conferring During Grapple Time

Let's break down the details of what might happen as you confer during Move 4: Ask. When you're ready to confer with a student, here are five steps for an efficient and purposeful conference.

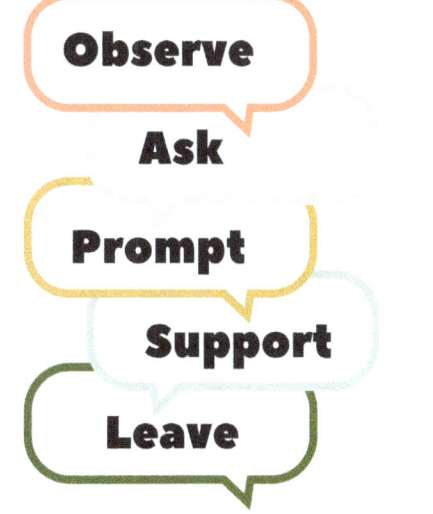

**Step 1: Observe**

The first thing I always do is pause to observe. Whether it's on the playground, during math, or when I see a conflict bubbling, I always start by observing. My guiding principle is: "Seek first to understand." Before making assumptions about what is happening, I take a moment to objectively observe the students' actions and think about what they might reveal.

Here's what I focus on observing:

- What is the student doing? Are they just sitting and thinking? Writing something down? If they are drawing or writing, what is it and is it helping them solve the problem?
- Are they making progress or are they stuck?
- Does their representation align with the problem?
- What mathematical reasoning is revealed in their work?

Observations set the foundation for a productive and tailored conference.

**Step 2: Ask**

Start with an open-ended question, like "Tell me about what you're doing." This opening is intentionally broad and does not imply how students should be using their Grapple Time or indicate a certain strategy they should be using. I avoid framing the opening as, "Show me how you're solving," because that might pressure a student who isn't solving yet. This approach allows students to share whatever is on their mind or describe what they are doing at that moment. Not every student is actively solving the problem or has a workable strategy, and that's okay. I want to use my questioning to normalize that experience and provide a safe space for students to share their thoughts.

Here are some other questions I might ask to begin a conference with a student:

- What are you up to?
- Can you tell me about your thinking?
- What's happening in your work so far?

**Step 3: Prompt**

Now it's time to prompt the students for more. A prompt serves two purposes: 1) you'll gain a better understanding of the student's thinking, and 2) the act of explaining often helps students clarify their own thinking. Explaining their mathematical reasoning often helps students better understand their choices and the reasoning behind their choices.

I use these two prompts most often:

1. Show/Tell me more about that [name I want to know more about].
2. Why did you do that? (Variations include: What in the story told you to do that? Why did you choose that manipulative? Why did you draw it this way?)

**Step 4: Support**

Once students have fully explained and you have a sense of their reasoning, it's time to decide if support is needed. Is it appropriate to offer the student a nudge or nugget to support or extend their thinking? Sometimes it's the right time and other times it is not. I use my intuition and the strategies I anticipated to guide this decision.

**Step 5: Leave**

After offering students a nudge or a nugget (or deciding to do neither), I walk away. Yep, I walk away. Why? Because it is much easier for students to apply new ideas without the pressure of an audience. I don't want to pressure students into implementing my idea, but rather I want them to choose what feels right to them. When we linger too long in the conference, it can feel like we're waiting for students to follow our instructions, which may lead to mimicking an idea just to please the teacher—even if they don't fully understand it or feel it's the best next move. We want students to think and make sense of problems, not just follow the leader.

## In Action: Four Moves to Facilitate Thinking During Grapple Time

Let's take a look at what the four moves within Grapple Time might look like in action.

In second grade students must solve addition and subtraction word problems demonstrating an understanding of place value, the properties of operations, and the relationship between addition and subtraction. In Amanda's class students are working toward this important grade-level skill and currently many students are using physical or visual strategies, like using or drawing base-ten blocks or cubes, to directly model addition and subtraction problems.

Within this broader understanding of addition and subtraction, Amanda chooses a learning goal that she believes is an important next step for her students: understand the change unknown problem type and use the relationship between addition and subtraction to add or subtract. The teacher anticipates students may do this through a variety of strategies including regrouping or decomposing the numbers to add or subtract in increments.

## Second Grade in October

**Task:**

*There are 52 children on the playground. A few more classes join them on the playground. Now there are 85 children on the playground. How many children were in the classes that joined?*

**Intended learning goal:**
Recognize the connection between addition and subtraction when solving a change unknown problem.

**Observations:**
During Grapple Time Amanda's observations unearthed some interesting thinking and areas of need among students. For example, the teacher noticed these three strategies:

- Alisha drew 52 in base-ten blocks and is drawing more tens and ones blocks to reach 85 in total (Figure G.9).

**FIGURE G.9** Alisha's work.

82  Word Problem Workshop

- Warner is counting up by tens, then by ones (Figure G.10).

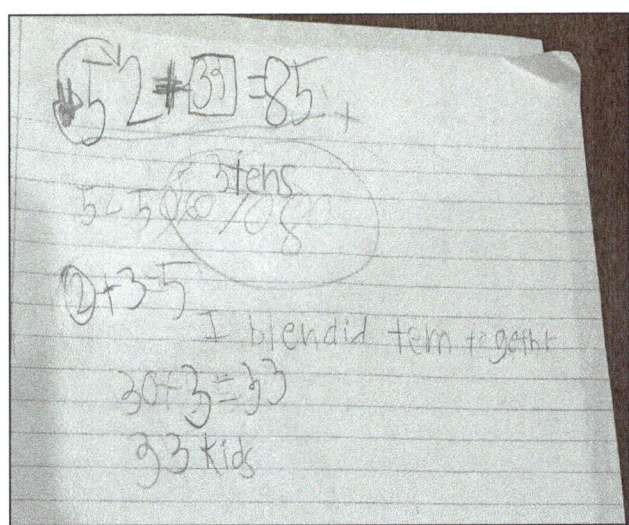

**FIGURE G.10** Warner's work.

- Raye is drawing base-ten blocks. She drew 85 using tens and ones and is starting to cross out 52, to subtract 52 from 85 (Figure G.11).

**FIGURE G.11** Raye's work.

Step 2: Grapple  83

- Timothy is breaking the numbers apart according to place value in order to subtract the tens, and then the ones (Figure G.12).

**FIGURE G.12** Timothy's work.

These four different strategies could all help highlight the learning goal and move students forward in their thinking. However, Amanda decides to learn more about the students' thinking before she selects strategies to focus on in the group discussion. In addition, she may choose other students to zone in on in order to offer nuggets or nudges to move their thinking along as well.

**Overall, Amanda notices:**

- Some students add up from 52 to 85 (52 + ? = 85).
- Some students decompose 52 and 85 by place value with number bonds or base-ten blocks.
- A few students subtract 52 from 85 (85 − 52 = ?).

**Amanda concludes:**

- It doesn't make sense to focus on the connection between addition and subtraction models today because only a couple of students saw subtraction as a solution pathway for this problem.
- Instead, she decides to focus on the connections between decomposing and using base-ten blocks.

**Amanda decides the class will discuss:**

- Warner's adding up with equations strategy (Figure G.10)

    $50 + 30 = 80$

    $80 + 2 = 82$ (this 2 being added is from the 52)

    $82 + 3 = 85$

    $30 + 3 = 33$ kids who came to the playground

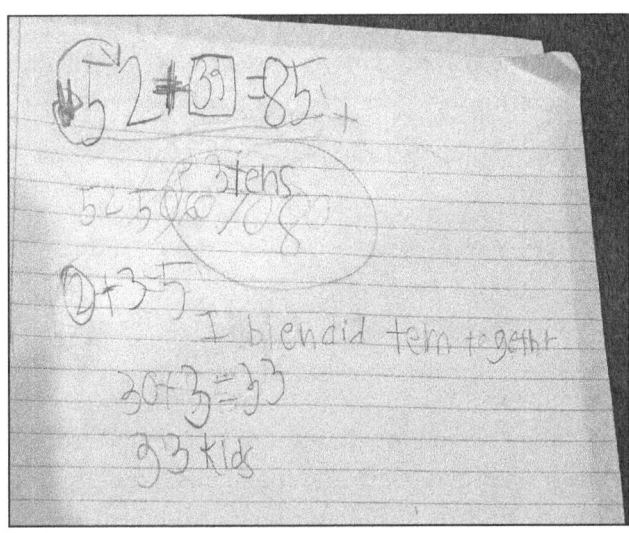

- Alisha's strategy of adding up using base-ten blocks (Figure G.9)

Amanda considers some possible questions to ask and prompts for the discussion:

- Compare the two strategies. Compare the representations of the strategies. "What do you notice is the same about these strategies? What is different about their models?"
- Link the model and strategies to the problem. "What in the problem told you to do that?" "Where are the 33 students that joined the playground?"
- "I wonder if these are the most efficient ways to solve this problem. What do you think?" "Which do you think is the most efficient?"

## Common Questions from Teachers

### What About When the Struggle Isn't Productive?

It is certain that somewhere along their math learning journey, students will get stuck, not know where to begin and make mistakes. All of these uncomfortable spots can be part of productive struggle, but at times, they're not. It's tough to engage in productive struggle when a student feels completely lost or defeated. When students are in a moment of unproductive struggle it is important that, instead of focusing on what they *can't* do, we point out what they *can* do. Help students understand that struggling is part of learning. They might not get the "right" answer immediately, or even today, but that's okay. The first step is helping students make sense of the problem. Encourage students to just start with what makes sense to *them*—using what they know. From there, we can scaffold and build on their understanding. It is all about shifting the focus from getting it perfect to getting it started, and from there, helping students grow through their struggles.

You might try these strategies to get students "unstuck" and back in a space of productive struggle:

- Reread the problem and support the student's understanding of the problem by asking them to retell it or asking them questions such as "What happens first in this story?"
- Suggest a first step. ("Can you draw the eighteen people?" "Can you use a number line to show 243?")

- Notice aloud what students can do. ("I see you're on the right track here with your representation. You started strong by decomposing these numbers.")

- Find what's frustrating a student and offer a nudge or nugget to address their road block ("Let's look back at yesterday's chart—do you see how Rosemary solved?" "Can you pass out the cookies to each of the plates? See, the problem says fifty cookies were put onto eight plates.")

- Send the student on a walk. The student can briefly walk around the classroom observing what others are trying to gain ideas for what they might be able to use in their problem solving.

## *What if Students Don't Solve at All?*

All behavior is communication. A brilliant social worker friend of mine, Meghan, taught me this foundational concept early in my career, and it is something I keep in mind when students are struggling to engage in grappling. When a student sits during work time and does nothing, it is concerning, and my instinct might be to convince them to get started. But instead of reacting right away, we can pause and consider what the student might be communicating by not engaging with or solving the problem. We can ask ourselves:

- What is their relationship with math class? With me? With their peers in this class? (Look back at your math surveys!)

- Might this student have a past experience (with math or something else) that is causing them to experience anxiety in relation to the task?

- How confident is this student in their abilities?

- How can I offer this student a way to get started that feels safe?

Instead of jumping in by telling them what to do, jump in with encouragement and relationship building. Try to remove any barriers that might be shutting them down—whether that means rereading the problem together or offering a quick pep talk and a suggestion for getting started.

One year I had a third-grade student, Kali, who would often shut down during Grapple Time. She would cry, crumple up papers and do anything she could think of to avoid solving the problem. I intentionally built a relationship with Kali outside of math time. I learned about her past experiences and discovered that her family always referred to her older sister as the "good-at-math sister," which led Kali to believe she wasn't good at math. Knowing this, I started offering small but consistent encouragement whenever I saw her making progress—nothing big, just a quick comment to acknowledge her as a mathematician. Over time, Kali began to engage more during Grapple Time and by the end of the first semester Kali went from blank papers every day to multiple strategies on her paper each day.

Here are some relationship-focused strategies you might try:

- Build relationships and learn about students' history with math.
- Notice and acknowledge their mathematician behaviors aloud to them.
- Offer short pep talks during Grapple Time (10–15 seconds).
- Instead of reacting by re-giving directions, respond by figuring out why they are not engaging.

## What if Students Run Out of Time and Do Not Finish Solving the Problem Before It Is Time to Share?

It is common for students to finish at different rates, with some completing tasks quickly and others still working at the end of the allotted time. You can adjust the amount of time allocated for Grapple Time each day, but it is important to also prepare extensions for students who finish early. Here are a few possible extensions:

- Solve the problem in at least two ways.
- Write in words how you solved the problem.
- Try the same problem again, but with different numbers.
- Write your own problem that is similar with different numbers (and maybe we will solve it as a class in the future!).

Once you have extended the time and provided tasks for early finishers, focus on understanding why some students are not finishing the task. Reflect on these questions:

- Are they using all their time?
- Are they actively working or distracted?
- Where are they struggling? Understanding the problem? Getting started? Continuing to solve once they've started down a solution pathway? Re-trying once they've hit a road block?

Spend time observing and conferring with students who do not finish to find out why. Then, provide support to those individuals. This support might come in the form of a small-group instruction to build conceptual understanding, more practice with strategies, or even providing a new seat and bin of manipulatives to help them stay engaged.

## How Many Math Conferences Can You Realistically Do in a Day?

Not many, and that's okay. Eventually over the course of a week, we will get to everyone. It is important to establish a system for who you talk to and when. I take notes on a template called the Forecasting Guide as a way to anticipate the strategies students will use and who might need support (more on this in the Planning for Word Problem Workshop chapter). Then I prioritize checking in with those students first. These students might be in need of extensions, support, or clarification. The needs of my students vary, so I keep track of my conferences and plan for future conferences based on students' needs.

## Is That Actually Enough Conferencing?

When I hear this question, I sense the teacher's deep concern and desire to meet their students' needs. We all want our students to succeed, and that often leads us to believe more is better. However, I really believe in quality over quantity. For example, a focused, three-minute conference with a student in which you're actively listening and engaging can be more impactful than trying to be "fully engaged" with all students at all times, which is neither realistic nor sustainable.

Grapple Time conferences are not the only opportunity to engage with students in math class. For example, even if I don't confer with a student on a particular day, I may engage with them during the Launch, listen in during a turn and talk in the Share or hear their thoughts during the whole-group Discussion.

## Will Some Students Need More Support?

Of course! We know that our students' needs vary and sometimes the just-in-time support in a conference isn't enough. In those cases, these students might need to come to the small-group table to solve a few more problems together or receive additional support in other ways.

# Be an Action Taker

## *First Steps*

- Set expectations for Grapple Time by making a chart like the one in Figure G.2.

- Set a timer for eight minutes for Grapple Time, and stick to it. Some students won't finish, but it will help you keep the pace and make time for all the steps of Word Problem Workshop.

- For the first two minutes of work time, observe your students without intervening. Then, ask open questions like, "What are you up to?" instead of giving advice. A nudge might be just what they need.

## *Ready to Run*

- Use the four moves to facilitate students' thinking—Scan, Walk, Zone In, Ask.

- Help students show their thinking clearly during Grapple Time by making a "Clear, Accurate, Precise" anchor chart (Figure G.4) with them.

- Set up your phone to record yourself during Grapple Time. Reflect on what you say to students during Grapple Time. Is your stance neutral? Are you giving students the space to think for themselves, or are you unintentionally stepping in too quickly?

# Step 3: Share

"I got it. I'm done," Trey said matter of factly before even walking back to his seat after the Launch. Trey was confident with strategies like compensating and decomposing—methods that many of his peers weren't even grappling with yet. He was confident in his mental math skills, but when it came time to pick up his pencil and record his thoughts, he froze.

"What do you mean you're done? You've got a blank paper, dude," I said, playfully trying to re-engage him with the problem.

"I have the answer, I don't need to write anything down" Trey persisted.

"What if you tell me what you did in your head and I write it down. You explain it and I'll show it on paper. Deal?"

"Fine," Trey sighed.

Each day of Word Problem Workshop, after Grapple Time, I chose two students to share their work at the front of the classroom. Sharing quickly became the most coveted job in class. Students stood proudly beside the easel, explaining their strategies as I scribed their work for everyone to see. These strategy charts stayed on display, inspiring others to try new approaches.

As the year progressed and the Share became a treasured daily routine in the classroom, Trey wanted to share. Initially skeptical of the need to record his ideas on paper, Trey began to see recording as a vehicle for engaging with his peers, something he was interested in. That desire to have his work highlighted too pushed him to start recording his ideas on paper. He began creating clear models and adding labels to show exactly how he solved problems in his head. Over time, Trey became a regular sharer, inspiring his classmates with strategies they may not have tried otherwise.

Word Problem Workshop didn't just help Trey overcome his challenges with recording his thinking—it gave him the confidence to share his ideas and illustrated how this sharing can inspire new ways of solving for the entire class.

> **We can** create opportunities for students to share their problem-solving approaches, make connections between strategies and ideas, and deepen their mathematical understanding.

## The Share

During the Share, students' models and strategies are shared with the whole class in order to spark a mathematical discussion. Students' work might inspire math discussions about the strategy a student used, how they modeled their strategy, the equations they wrote or their reasoning. The students' work becomes part of the evidence students cite during the discussion. There are five parts to efficiently and effectively sharing students' work so that everyone is positioned to discuss the work and learn from others' perspectives. They include:

1. Preparing the space
2. Selecting who will share
3. Positioning everyone for the Share
4. Scribing the Share
5. Engaging every student

> **Goals of the Share**
> - Support students in sharing their strategies and ideas
> - Engage students in listening to understand others' strategies and ideas
> - Develop connections between the strategies and approaches shared
> - Create a shared experience for all students to draw from during the Discussion (Step 4)

## Prepare the Space

First, you'll want to prepare the classroom space and materials so the Share is streamlined and impactful in engaging all students in thinking together about the math. Determine a space in your classroom where students can gather around a piece of chart paper or whiteboard where you will scribe the students' work. The space should be big enough for all the students to sit facing the chart or in a circle. I prefer to use the carpet in the meeting area of my classroom. You should also determine a space where the students sharing will sit or stand so that the class can see both the sharer and their work as it is scribed.

Prepare the chart paper to scribe the students' strategies and models. Write or tape a large copy of the problem on the chart paper so it can be easily referred back to in the discussion. Also, leave a few colored markers near the board or easel with which to record students' thinking. Although simple, these pre-prepared materials will help your Share go smoothly when transitioning students from Grapple Time to the Share.

## Select Who Will Share

Prior to coming to the gathering space for the Share you'll have already made key observations during Grapple Time that will inform your next moves. Before the Share begins, you will select which students will share their work and decide the order in which they will share. The goal is to choose students' reasoning, strategies, and representations that will help illuminate and spark discussion around the learning goal you planned. Based on your observations and conferences, choose two or three students to share their work with the class. In the Planning for Word Problem Workshop chapter we will discuss how to select learning goals for Word Problem Workshop.

When considering who to select to share ask yourself:

- What strategies or models did the majority of students use?
- Did someone uncover a new idea during Grapple Time that needs to be discussed?
- Which strategies might align best with the learning goal?
- Is there an approach that is new to this class?
- Are there strategies that students can compare?

## Ordering the Shares

Deciding the order in which students will share is often based on how you plan to structure the Share.

- Will students compare and contrast the strategies or models?
- Will you choose strategies that build in sophistication, complexity, or efficiency?
- Will you choose a third strategy to share that might not be the main focus of the discourse, but is there in case you need an extension or support?
- Do you want to create a debate?

When in doubt, start with the most familiar strategy and then introduce a strategy that is less familiar to your students.

Once you've narrowed down your selected students and the order in which they will share, be sure the students are prepared to share. Quickly check in with each sharer before coming to the gathering space to ensure they are prepared to present their ideas. Give them a heads up that they will share so that they have a few minutes to quickly rehearse. You can do this by putting a sticky note with a 1 or 2 on their desk. This lets the student know they will be the first or second sharer. You might prompt them by saying, "You're going to share this portion of your strategy today. Are you ready to explain what you did and why you did it?"

## How Do You Choose the Students to Share?

Choosing who will share on any given day is a balancing act of many factors including what the students in the class already know and can do, new strategies to nudge them forward in their understanding, the learning goal you planned for, students' social-emotional needs, and more. You'll want to lean on your observations to see what strategies students are using and what you've forecasted. Taking notes on the Forecasting Guide can help you identify trends in the strategies used that day, and over the course of a week. We will explore this work further in the Planning for Word Problem Workshop chapter, where we'll look at how we can use forecasting to plan what students might do and which work we might select for the Share.

When I select who will share I like to choose one strategy that I notice most students can use and understand. This allows every child to engage in the Share because there is at least one strategy they understand and with which they can connect. By sharing a familiar strategy that many students likely used to solve the problem, I can select a student who really needs a confidence boost or who worked really hard that day.

However, it is important to make sure the selected students' math work aligns with the learning goal. Always choose shares based on mathematical thinking, not to "make it fair." Word Problem Workshop is a time commitment, and the student work is essential to advancing everyone's understanding. The Share is not the time to give in to students begging to share. Instead, maintain high expectations for sharers—observe their solving strategies, ask them about their thinking, and select only those whose strategies support the learning goal. Sharing will become a sought after opportunity in the math community and students will work hard during Grapple Time to earn a spot to share. Hold the students to high expectations of sharing: a solid strategy, clear reasoning, and readiness to explain loud and proud.

Let's take a look at some ways the Share looks in action!

### In Action: Preparing the Share

I chose three students to share their approach to the problem (Figure S.1):

*4 students share 6 brownies equally so each student gets the same amount. How much does each student get?*

**Learning goal:** Understand the equivalence among approaches to equally share. Consider the question: Are these all the same amount?

**Selected:** I chose three students to share who each had a different solving approach that linked to the learning goal. I planned to have students compare and contrast the strategies to reason about equivalence. I hoped students might compare N's and S's strategies to see how they arrived at the same answer. I was unsure of students' level of understanding of fractions and equivalence so I also added J's strategy with fourths to allow for a conversation about equivalence between two-fourths and one-half. This variety of strategies allowed me to make in-the-moment decisions in the discussion based on what the students noticed and what they understood. (More on this decision making later in this chapter.)

**Order:** This is order of sharers/strategies I chose:

- **Student 1 "N":** Passed out a whole brownie to each of the four students. Then split the remaining two brownies into halves and gave each student a half, resulting in $1\frac{1}{2}$ brownies for each student.

**FIGURE S.1** Three students' (N, J, and S) strategies for sharing 6 brownies equally between 4 students.

- **Student 2 "J":** Also passed out a whole brownie to each student, but split the remaining two brownies into fourths and gave each student two fourths. Their answer was $1\frac{2}{4}$ brownies for each student.
- **Student 3 "S":** Split all the brownies into halves and passed out the halves to the four students. Resulting in each student getting three halves or $1\frac{1}{2}$ brownies.

I ordered the strategies from the one with which the class would be most familiar (N's strategy) to strategies that might be less familiar to some students (J's and S's strategies). As students listened to the sharers they began to notice connections between the three strategies as well as noticing equivalencies ($\frac{1}{2} + \frac{1}{2} + \frac{1}{2} = 1\frac{1}{2}$ and $\frac{2}{4} = \frac{1}{2}$). They were ready to engage in a robust discussion!

## Challenges with Choosing a Sharer

Selecting student work to share is a complex decision with many factors to consider. Sometimes the chosen work leads to a rich discussion; other times, making connections between strategies and ideas may be more challenging. There are many reasons why things don't always go as planned. However, by choosing a worthy task, aligning it with a meaningful learning goal, and forecasting potential strategies, you'll be prepared to make effective selections based on your observations.

## Collaboration to Choose Sharers

If there are other adults in your classroom, it is helpful to briefly confer with them before selecting and ordering sharers. Task these educators with talking with students and observing during Grapple Time. Then, take thirty seconds to huddle up with the other adults to discuss who will share that day and how their work connects to the learning goal.

If you don't have another adult in your class, invite your math coach or colleagues to stop by on occasion. I especially love using learning labs (Figure S.2), a classroom-embedded structure for professional development in which a group of teachers study and make instructional decisions collaboratively such as selecting shares together. As a group, we listen to student thinking, then quickly huddle up to decide who will share. Aligning our ideas around how to get as many students as we can to the learning goal through strategically choosing which students to share helps everyone improve. Inevitably a teacher will notice some aspect of student thinking that others missed, and we all learn together.

**FIGURE S.2** A huddle to confer with the teachers visiting my classroom during a learning lab. We each shared our observations and possible shares that aligned to the learning goal.

# Position Everyone for the Share

Prepare for the Share by clearly defining everyone's role during this part of the Word Problem Workshop. You step into the roles of facilitator and scribe, the class takes on the role of the listeners, and the selected students become the teachers, presenting their ideas to the group.

## Position the Sharer

Selected students share their strategies and ideas with the class for later discussion. They explain the steps they took to solve the problem, describing the reasoning behind their decisions. Each sharer has the spotlight to teach the class about their mathematical ideas and process for solving the problem. Have the students who are not sharing at the moment sit or stand near the chart so they can focus on both the sharer and their work. To guide students' attention I prompt by saying, "Your eyes should be on the sharer's face or their work up here."

Before the sharer begins, I remind them to tell the class *what they did* and *why they did it*, referencing our class chart (Figure S.3) as a visual reminder. A student sharing their strategy for the problem in Figure S.4 using the *what I did/why I did it* framework might sound like this: "First I drew a box to show a foot. I did this because Lauren planted a seed every $\frac{3}{4}$ of a foot, so I needed to make the foot. Then, I partitioned the foot into fourths by drawing lines straight down. Next I labeled them $\frac{1}{4}, \frac{2}{4}, \frac{3}{4}, \frac{4}{4}$. I did that to help me keep track of where $\frac{3}{4}$ would be in each foot. So I put a dot to show the seed at $\frac{3}{4}$."

**FIGURE S.3** This classroom poster with prompts helps students prepare to share their ideas. I place it near the math area so they can refer to it during their Share.

## Position the Students as Listeners

Position the rest of the class as the audience for the sharer's ideas. The students should face the sharer, ready to listen and think critically about the sharer's ideas. Use phrases like, "show *us*" or "tell *us* what you did," to remind students that the sharer is speaking to the class, not just the teacher. Encourage sharers to speak to their peers directly. If needed, gently prompt with, "Great! Don't tell me, tell your audience," while gesturing toward the class.

## Position Yourself as the Scribe

**FIGURE S.4** The teacher scribes the sharers' strategies as they explain to the class *what they did* and *why they did it*.

Position yourself as the scribe. Record the sharers' strategies and models on a large piece of chart paper or the whiteboard (Figure S.5), ensuring everyone can easily see and refer back to the work. Limit how much you speak to keep the focus on the student sharing their ideas.

The scribe role is an adult responsibility, as you will be able to record efficiently and clearly, allowing students to focus on listening and thinking. Outside of Word Problem Workshop, you can provide other opportunities for students to record their thinking on whiteboards and create posters.

**FIGURE S.5** The student takes the lead in explaining their process and reasoning while the teacher scribes and the class listens.

## Scribe the Share

With the sharers selected and everyone in position, it is time for the main event—getting students' strategies and models drawn up where everyone can see them! The Share begins by asking the first sharer to "Tell us what you did and why you did it." This prompt encourages the student to share each step they took to solve and the reasoning behind it. As the scribe you will ensure students fully explain their steps so you can record them, while keeping the pace of the Share swift enough to keep the class's attention.

## Three Things to Say as You Scribe

There are three helpful things to say (and do!) as you scribe and as each student shares. Let's go through each one and the reasoning behind why these are essential elements to share and scribe.

### "Tell Us What You Did and Why You Did It"

Use this simple yet powerful prompt with students during the Share. It sets students up to explain their thinking without you having to interrupt much. The goal is for the student to fully explain their thinking. Of course, they may need help along the way to explain more, clarify, or even to slow down. However, for the sake of engagement and efficiency encourage students to share their ideas without teacher commentary.

Encourage the class to listen to the sharer by centering their voice. Repeating what students say is tempting, but establishes a habit of students listening to

**FIGURE S.6** A representation of teacher talk (orange lines) and student talk (black line) during the Share.

only the teacher, and not building their skills of listening to one another. By reducing your comments during this time it forces students to listen to understand what the sharer is saying. This further reinforces the notion that the sharer is the expert and the class is the audience working to understand the sharer's thinking. You'll notice in Figure S.6 that the teacher limits their comments to prompts that ask the sharer for more information in order to scribe accurately. In this representation the black line represents the times the sharer is speaking, while the orange lines represent when the teacher prompts the student for more information. Notice the long chunks of time in which the student is talking uninterrupted.

## "What Equation Goes with Your Strategy? What Equation Matches the Problem?"

Writing equations is a skill practiced in isolation in many curricula. Curriculum tasks typically ask students to read a problem and write an equation or to find all the equations that match a certain problem situation. Although these are great ways to practice understanding equations, I find that embedding writing equations into our daily Word Problem Workshop routine helps students see the relevance of an equation.

We focus on two types of equations in Word Problem Workshop. First is an equation that matches the problem and the second is an equation that matches how a student solved it. At times these equations may be the same, and at other times they may be different. During each share I ask the student to give the equation that matches their work and the equation that matches the problem which I record alongside their model and strategy.

To teach students how to write equations that match problems I suggest the following:

1. Start by doing it together after the shares. Write a line under the problem that will house the equation that matches the problem. Eventually you will move to students doing this independently, but this is a good way to begin to learn the skill.

2. Reread the problem and write down the numbers in the order they appear in the problem.

3. Reason about the context and how it relates to the numbers. In Figure S.7 you see there are 14 groups of an unknown number of students with a total of 98 students. Ask students to think about

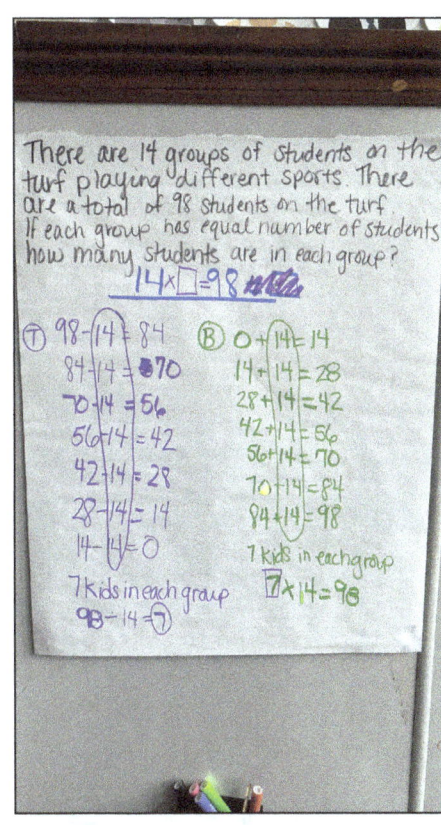

**FIGURE S.7** A chart shows Student T's strategy in purple (on the left side of the chart) and Student B's strategy in green (on the right side of the chart). Both students also shared an equation that matched their strategy.

these numbers and the words in the problem to determine what operations might match the context.

4. Avoid circling or indicating keywords. Keywords do not always work to help our students figure out how to solve or create an equation. For example, the word "left" is often a "keyword" for subtraction—"How much is left?" However, this isn't always the case; the word "left" can be used in different contexts, with different meanings other than subtraction. Take this problem for example: *Ben left $3 on the table for a tip. Erin left $5 more on the table for a tip. How much money was left on the table for a tip?* In this case, assuming "left" is a signal to subtract without understanding the context of the problem will result in a wrong answer.

FIGURE S.8 Darious, a third grader, uses direct modeling and repeated addition to solve a problem. He demonstrates connections between an addition equation he used to solve and a multiplication equation that matches the problem type.

Figures S.8 and S.9 are student work examples that illustrate ways in which students connect word problems to equations.

Number modeling or writing equations to match a situation is a skill that evolves over time. As students practice each day they start to see connections between different problem contexts and the equations that can represent them. For example, in Figure S.9 the student shows evidence of noticing a part-part-whole relationship in the word problem when they record $104 = ? + 78$. He also recorded an equation that matches his strategy, which was starting at 78 and

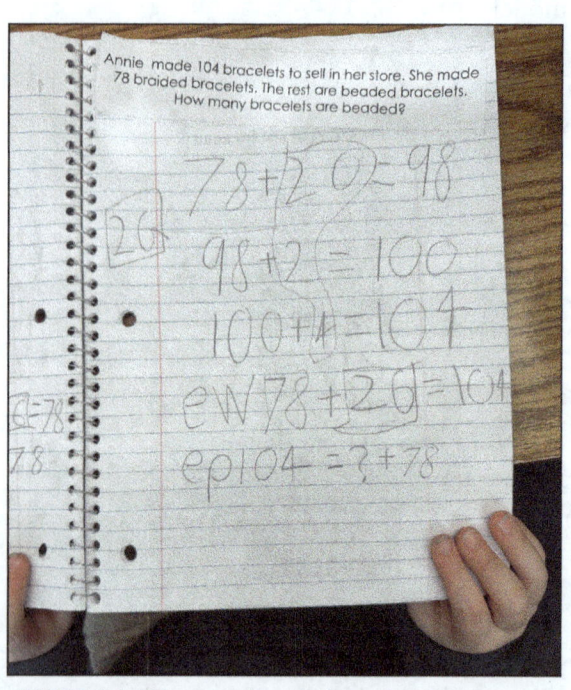

FIGURE S.9 This second grader's teacher has a norm for students to write "ew" for an equation that represents their strategy and "ep" for an equation that matches the context of the problem.

adding up 26 to result in 104. These nuanced differences help students make sense of problems and deepen their strategic reasoning. Your expectations for students' equations will vary based on your grade-level standards. However, students at all grade levels can start to practice writing equations.

## "What Is Your Answer Statement?"

The final step of the Share is the answer statement. The student gives the answer statement by answering the question in the problem. It might sound like this:

> TEACHER: So, Lana, how many cars went through the car wash?
> LANA: Twenty-seven cars went through the car wash.

Making sure students give a clear answer statement reinforces the idea that students are answering a question in a story, not just getting a numerical answer. Asking for an answer statement also ensures students are thinking about the units and context of their answer. Lana responded with "twenty-seven cars." If she had just said, "twenty-seven," then her teacher might prompt her with a bit of humor, replying, "twenty-seven crocodiles?" (or insert some other ridiculous noun!). This usually reminds students to respond with the correct unit.

## Scribe a Clear, Accurate, and Precise Model

As you scribe, consider this an opportunity to model how to create accurate, precise, and clear models for students. That might mean you stray slightly from how the student represented it on their paper, but not entirely.

For example, if a student uses a number line but didn't accurately partition it into fourths, you can record an equally partitioned number line as you scribe their strategy (Figure S.10). Or if a student uses an open number line to show addition, but the +30 is the same size as +10 (Figure S.11), you should make the jumps proportional when you record the strategy for the class (Figure S.12). We can model how to create more accurate and precise models.

**FIGURE S.10** A student approximates partitioning a number line into fourths. When the teacher scribes this strategy they have the opportunity to emphasize partitioning equally.

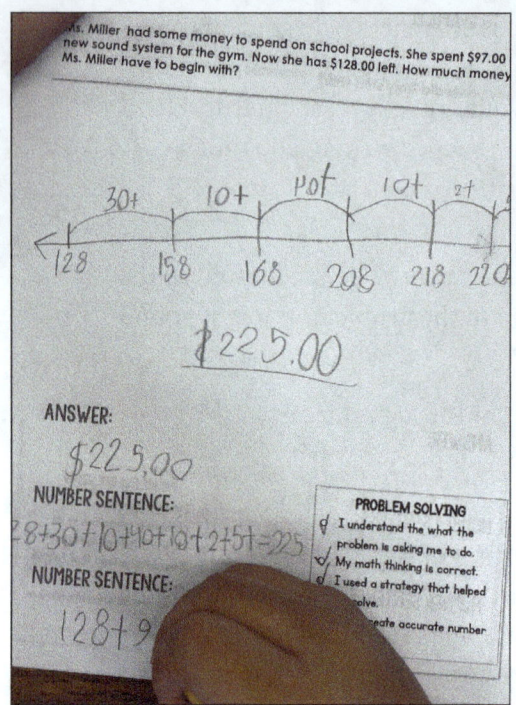

**FIGURE S.11** A student creates an open number line where +30 is the same distance as +10. When scribing, the teacher can model how to make these jumps proportional.

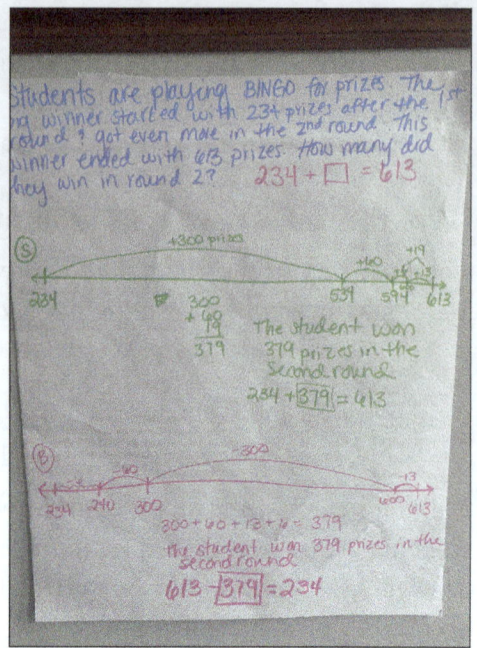

**FIGURE S.12** A teacher scribes an open number line that shows the +300 jump longer than the +60 jump. Although the student may not have done this as precisely on their paper, the teacher can use the Share to point out the importance of an accurate and precise model.

On another student's work, maybe the equations are unorganized and written all over the page. You'll scribe by lining them up to create a clearer model that viewers can better understand. You might say, "I'm going to go ahead and put that next equation right under this one you just described. That way it will be clear and easy to follow your ideas." You will not represent the work in a totally different way than the student did, but instead just enhance their work as needed to model a clear, accurate, and precise representation.

Charts of students' strategies serve as an important student resource for the math community (Figures S.13 and S.14). Leave the posters hanging in a predictable spot in your room so students can refer back to the strategies they shared on previous days. You can also use the chart to connect ideas in future discussions: "Remember when Maya solved using a number line and it was efficient because she could make those big hops and little hops," or "Look back at Sam's strategy from yesterday. How is that the same or different from what Madhav did here?"

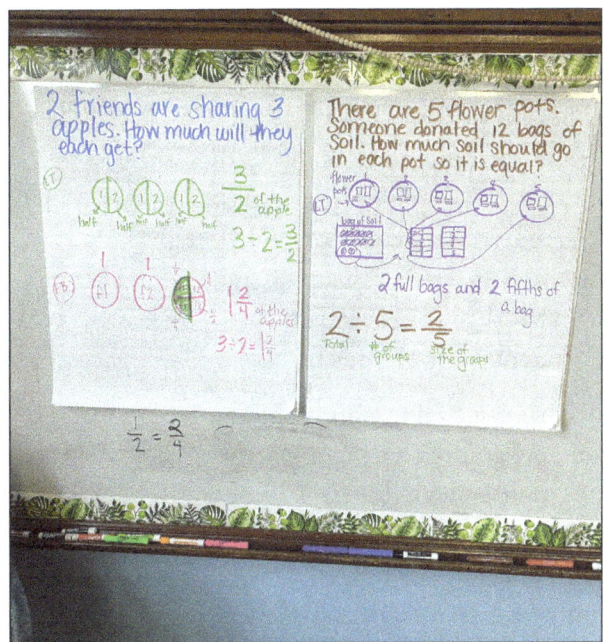

**FIGURE S.13** Grouping math charts together helps students refer back to previous strategies they have used or learned from classmates. I suggest creating a "math area" on the walls or boards of your classroom where the Word Problem Workshop share chart can live as well as any anchor charts or criteria lists you create together.

**FIGURE S.14** I leave charts up for students to refer back to. To save space I leave up the previous two days' shares. Then I put the new day's problem on top of the oldest share. This ensures what we discussed yesterday is always up in a place where students can access and refer back to it.

### Scribing Tips

- Make sure to leave enough room on your paper or chart so that all the sharers' strategies fit.
- Use one color to represent each student's thinking. Since students only have a pencil (one color) this is a good way to model using numbers and labels to accurately represent thinking.
- Use a different color for each student to distinguish between the students' work.

## Maintaining Engagement During the Share

The Share is the perfect time to teach students how to listen and learn from one another. Sometimes it takes a while to share and students' attention gets off track. These five strategies can help students actively listen to the student sharing.

1. **Give them something to think about.** Before students begin to share I'll say, "Today I want you to listen for: (fill in the blank with what you want them to pay attention to such as "the decisions the student made," "how manipulatives were used to solve," or "the connections between this strategy and the first one"). This strategy works for many parts of Word Problem Workshop. However, I really like to use this strategy any time students' main job is to listen.

2. **Be error detectives.** Mistakes happen during the Share, and when they do we all help each other fix them. As you're sharing a strategy a student might describe something that is incorrect. It is okay to still record the student's idea and task your students with finding the error. Of course, you'll want to make sure to have norms and expectations for how to respectfully find errors and assist each other in fixing them.

3. **Be the Best Active Listener.** This is a fun strategy that works with almost every class because it's a *mild* competition. Designate a student to keep an eye out for the Best Active Listener. This will need to be someone who is meeting all the established norms for active listening. Then, after the Share, the student will reveal the Best Active Listener and we will give them a quick cheer to celebrate their listening!

4. **Make connections.** Eventually we will ask students to discuss connections between the strategies shared and their own strategy. Prompting students to notice connections while they are listening to the sharer is a great way to keep them engaged in listening and thinking. You might say something like, "Now we are going to hear from Georgette. I want you to look for connections between her strategy and Zoe's," or "After this we are going to discuss how your own strategy was the same or different as Megha and Emme's. Be thinking about that as you hear them describe their strategy." These prompts give students a reason to listen closely.

5. **Signal that you're listening.** Teach students signals to show their thoughts as they listen. We can all relate to having a hard time waiting to share a great idea. Using signals gives students a way to communicate that they have an idea without interrupting the sharer. Introduce one signal at a time and give students time to

practice using the signal. It might sound like, "Today when you have an idea that builds on something being shared use the Build Signal from American Sign Language to let us know you can build on their idea. It looks like this." Introducing the signals one at a time will allow students to try them out and find success with them before trying out another. Soon you'll have three or four signals that students are comfortable using. Other signals you might use are: I agree/me too; I have a different thought/I disagree; brain match/connection; I found a pattern; I found a mistake.

## Common Questions from Teachers

### What if There Are No Strategies to Share?

This happens. Sometimes the problem is too difficult for most students and they struggle to access the problem. You will likely notice that students are unproductively struggling during Grapple Time. In these cases, you can pause to make adjustments to the numbers, context, or number of steps in the problem to help students get back on track.

However, if students continue to struggle, even after these adjustments, you can shift what you're looking to select to share. Start by identifying the barriers students are facing.

- Is it the multiple steps?
- Is it the math concepts or procedures?
- Is it the size of the numbers?
- Is it the context of the problem?

Keep in mind that there is no one perfect way to deal with this situation. However, I encourage you to look at student work to see what *could* be shared. Ask one student to share part of their strategy and another to share just their equations. Maybe two students could work together to explain if they used the same strategy.

### What if No One Got It Right? Can I Share a Wrong Answer?

It is okay to share a correct strategy that results in the wrong answer. Sharing a wrong answer or strategy with mistakes can also be powerful. In Word

Problem Workshop we are more focused on understanding the problem's context and how it relates to the student's strategy and model than we are on the answer alone.

We have much to learn from the student who fully understood the problem and solved it, but made some calculation errors. In fact, that's the perfect thing to coach a potential sharer on before you select. You might see a student with a shareable strategy, but they have several errors. You might say, "I would love you to share this with the class, but first I want you to look back at this" and point to the problem area. Then walk away and check back on the student in a minute. Whether or not they were able to find and correct the error, you can still invite them to share by saying, "Are you willing to share that as a work in progress? I can help you through the small errors you've made while you share. Is that okay with you?" Prior to sharing you want the student to know that you are sharing their work that does not yet result in a correct answer and get their approval.

As always, you'll want to weigh your selections for the Share based on your learning goal and which strategies will move the class toward deepening their understanding most. Sometimes that means sharing a common error, especially if many students in the class made the same mistake. This could be an opportunity for students to identify and correct the error collaboratively.

## *What if Students Are Getting Stuck Using the Same Strategies Over and Over?*

While many students develop new and more sophisticated strategies over time through class conversations and strategic practice, some seem to get "stuck" using the same strategy over and over, even when it is no longer efficient or does not make sense for the numbers. For example, while counting on to solve 9 + 2 is a reasonable strategy, counting on by ones to solve 998 + 234 is not. In cases where you might want to give students a nudge to try a new strategy, consider introducing "The Way I Solved." Rather than relying on just your own students' strategies, you can introduce a strategy you want to highlight—naming it as your own or the strategy of a student from a previous year. Together the class can analyze the strategy, figure out how to use it and how it works, and then try it out for themselves.

To do this, chart the new strategy on large paper and present it at the Share. You can say something like, "Mr. T was telling me about one way his class solved this problem and I want to share it with you. First they…" and then continue to share the strategy. Sprinkling these types of shares in once in a while helps encourage students to try different strategies or models they haven't yet considered.

My favorite example of "The Way I Solved" in action is when I wanted to encourage students to think about compensation strategies for addition. They understood the strategy when doing number talks and problem strings, but they rarely applied it when solving word problems independently. Finally I said, "Friends, I have to show you how my mom does this kind of problem in her head. Back when I was in fifth grade like you, she told me her secret for figuring out prices at the grocery store so fast in her head. When a price says something like $6.97 she just added three pennies to make it $7.00, then added it to the cost of whatever else she was buying. In the end, she subtracted the three pennies she had added to the $6.97. Let me show you." My students' faces lit up like actual light bulbs—huge smiles and audible ohhhs. Next thing you know they were trying out compensation strategies in their own problems wherever they could!

You may also have lessons in your curriculum that introduce strategies which can nudge students toward applying different strategies to their problem solving. While I encourage you to keep Word Problem Workshop time open to allow students to use any strategy that makes sense to them, you might remind students that they can draw on the strategies they have been learning and using during the rest of math time.

## What Should I Do When a Student Is Taking a Long Time to Explain Their Strategy?

While I don't suggest stopping between shares, typically, if the Share is taking several minutes I will stop and ask students to turn and talk about what they have heard so far. This gives students a few seconds to "download" what they heard the student sharing and gives them a movement/talk break before refocusing for the next share.

For longer shares I suggest:

- Asking the student to be concise and clear in their words: "Just tell us what you did next," "Why?" "Next?"
- Refraining from asking clarifying questions or enacting talk moves during the Share
- Inserting a turn and talk between shares to give students a break

# Be an Action Taker

## *First Steps*

- Set up a space in your classroom to meet together as a whole group (preferably in a circle) where students can present their strategies.

- Find some Mr. Sketch smelly markers so your share is extra fun! (But any markers will do!) Keep them next to your chart paper where you've prepared the problem so you're ready to chart students' strategies.

- Find a space on your walls to keep your math posters so students can refer back to them.

## *Ready to Run*

- Improve students' engagement during the Share by using the five engagement strategies shared on pages 105–106.

- Center your students' voices by limiting your interjections during the Share. Limit your prompts to "Tell us why?" and "What did you do next?"

- Choose two students to share, and scribe their strategies on a piece of chart paper! Then send me a picture of your chart and tell me how it went! (Find me on social media at @hellomonamath or email me at hellomonamath@gmail.com)

# Step 4: Discuss

*"Good Student. Talks too much!"* graced nearly every single report I got as a student.

My gift of the gab is a trait I see as an asset of my outgoing personality, making me unafraid to engage with new people or get the party started by striking up a conversation. However, my desire to engage in conversation wasn't always welcomed in my classrooms as a student (Figure D.1). When I became a teacher I knew I wanted something different for my students. I wanted a classroom full of discussion, space for kids like me to process their thoughts through talking, and space for students who might not feel comfortable chatting at first to grow as both talkers and listeners.

Not surprisingly though, as a teacher, I found myself continuing to "talk too much" when what I really wanted was students to "talk too much." I knew I needed to focus my efforts on developing a classroom community where students' voices drove conversations and my voice was reserved for questions and prompts that got students to participate, share more, and think deeper. I realized I needed to quiet my own voice in order to amplify my students' voices. Over time, I started to see my role in discussions very differently, and I now make it my personal mission to "listen too much" and talk much less.

Do you also like the idea of a classroom full of discussions, and believe in the potential of these conversations to help students crystallize their understanding of mathematics? I'm guessing, if you're reading this chapter, the

**FIGURE D.1** Me as a little one, always ready for a conversation!

answer might be yes! But if we're being honest, facilitating these kinds of discussions, even when we believe in them wholeheartedly, can feel challenging. Math discussions can quickly go off the rails. Comments might wander far from the learning goal. One student's incorrect reasoning can confuse the entire group. What starts as an attempt to let students reason their way forward can quickly become you, the teacher, steering the conversation entirely. You may have entered the discussion with the best intentions, to let students take the lead while you facilitate, but somewhere along the way, you might find yourself doing most of the talking. You might start to question: Is this worth the time and effort?

The challenges of facilitating a math discussion are real and can be frustrating at times, but they highlight a deeper question that is important to reflect on.

### Who is doing the talking and thinking?

As teachers, it can be tempting to drive the discussions, asking leading questions like, "What should I do next?" or "So now we have… because we…," which prompt students to fill in the blanks rather than share their own ideas. In my own classroom these kinds of questions gave the illusion that students were thinking and even felt productive in the moment. But often my students were just parroting my own ideas back to me. Fill-in-the-blank questions don't build the reasoning or communication skills our students need in order to truly understand math. Instead, they position us as the expert and students as passive participants, missing an opportunity for students to do the thinking. To make discussions worthwhile, we must confront these challenges and rethink how we facilitate discussions, ensuring that students—not teachers—are doing the important work of explaining and reasoning.

> **We can** guide students to engage in rich discussions, sharing their own mathematical reasoning, while also learning from peers' perspectives in order to build deeper mathematical understanding.

## Never Skip the Discussion—It's Worth the Time!

You might be surprised at how much talking about your thinking can deepen your understanding. Math discussions give students the opportunity to share, reflect, and deepen their mathematical understanding through metacognition. Metacognition is when you pay attention to how you think and learn. Discussing your math reasoning helps you be metacognitive because you have the opportunity to explain your ideas and processes out loud. When you do this, you can check if your ideas make sense, notice mistakes, and figure out what strategies are working. It's like listening to your brain and considering, "Why did I do it this way?" Participating in math discussions helps students work through their own process of solving and understanding the math.

Research consistently underscores the importance of classroom discussions as one of the most impactful ways to improve learning. In his book, *Visible Learning*, John Hattie outlines his research that shows that classroom discussions have an effect size of 0.82, significantly higher than the 0.40 hinge point he uses to identify practices that positively impact learning (2009). Discussions create a space for students to reflect on their problem-solving choices and the reasoning behind them. When students think about what they did, why they did it, and how they might improve next time, they develop metacognitive skills that allow them to approach future problems with confidence and purpose.

When students discuss their reasoning and compare it to the reasoning of others, they learn to articulate their ideas clearly and thoughtfully. This process doesn't just help them understand the math they're working on; it builds critical communication skills. Skills learned in the math discussion extend beyond the math classroom. Skills like listening to others' perspectives, evaluating ideas, and connecting new ideas with existing ideas prepare students to communicate throughout their lives.

> **Goals of the Discussion**
> - Engage in discussing and justifying math thinking
> - Ask questions and engage with others' reasoning
> - Engage with peers' work as the foundation for rich conversation
> - Build deeper mathematical understanding through frequent discussions

## Discussions Are Like Campfires

As I've shared before, I spent many years camping with students. Every year, we'd load onto the buses with our students and drive out of the city, venturing into nature, eventually gathering around a campfire each evening to sing songs and make s'mores. Campfires have a unique way of bringing people together, sparking joy and bringing a sense of comfort. To me, gathering around a campfire for a chat is a special experience, much like circling up with my students in math class. Let's take a look at some of the similarities between campfires and math discussions (Figures D.2 and D.3).

I'll be honest with you, I'm not an expert campfire builder, but I'm always working on it. Some days, I start a roaring fire that lasts, impressing myself with how well I've put everything together. Other days, despite following the same routine, the fire won't start or flickers out quickly. This mirrors my facilitation of discussions—sometimes my questions spark lively student thinking, while other times it's like pulling teeth to get students talking. A poorly placed log can stifle a fire, just as a poorly framed question can hinder the flow of ideas. Sometimes, we just have to give ourselves grace, be patient, and keep trying.

| Campfire | Math Discussion |
|---|---|
| **Safe environment** that must be carefully maintained to ensure the fire stays manageable and contained | **Classroom community** in which students feel supported and free to take risks |
| **Heat** sources spark the start of the fire | **Student work** shared sparks the discussion and gets it going |
| **Fuel** keeps the fire burning | **Questions** keep the discussion going, sparking new connections |
| **Oxygen** sustains the chemical reaction that keeps the fire alive | **Students' math thinking** is the essential element that makes the discussion productive |
| **Structure** of the logs allows air to circulate and maintain the flame | **Structure** of the Discussion Framework allows students' conversation and ideas to circulate |

**FIGURE D.2** How campfires are similar to math discussions.

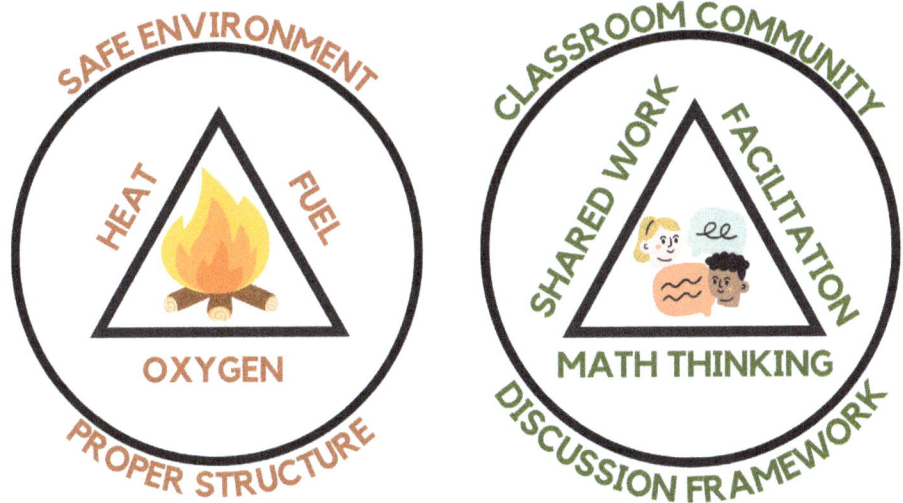

**FIGURE D.3** Campfires are like discussions, each piece working together to ensure success.

## What Makes a Good Math Discussion?

A good math discussion is driven by students' reasoning and guided by a skillful facilitator keen to keep students' thinking centered. The goal for a math discussion is to provide a space for students to work through their thinking and hear the perspectives of others doing the same. That means students' voices must be prioritized, allowing students the opportunity to participate by sharing their own mathematical ideas. Good discussions help students build ownership of their learning by explaining their thinking, building on others' ideas, and forming new mathematical insights.

For discussions to be meaningful, students need something to discuss, which is why in Word Problem Workshop the Discussion always follows Grapple Time and the Share. Grapple Time allows students to work through problems and form ideas to share. In the Share, the sharers explain their reasoning, leading to the Discussion, where all students look for connections, consider others' perspectives, and explore mathematical patterns and truths. A good math discussion provides students motivation for solving word problems. In the end, we get to sit down with our community and hash out our ideas.

While math discussions can take many paths, ultimately strong discussions are:

- Grounded in students' mathematical thinking
- Inclusive of all students' voices and perspectives
- Structured to keep students engaged and thinking
- Centered on a learning goal

Within these strong discussions, you'll find students and teachers each contributing to their success in a variety of ways.

**What students do in strong discussions:**

- Have the autonomy to contribute, ask questions and build on ideas that make sense to them
- Build on and connect ideas shared by classmates

**What teachers do in strong discussions:**

- Focus students' attention on mathematical models and strategies
- Help students identify patterns and make conjectures
- Help students make connections to previously discussed ideas
- Encourage students to engage by speaking and listening

# Facilitating Engagement in the Discussion

When students are excited to participate, math discussions come alive. Here are six suggestions to make that goal a reality.

## 1) Circle Up

During math discussions we sit in a circle so that each member of the conversation can be seen and heard. I like to think about circling up like a group of friends gathering around at a book club. It would not be very conducive to conversation if they arranged their chairs behind one another in rows! They wouldn't be able to chat, acknowledge one another, or hear from each friend. Instead, the book club friends gather in a circle so that each person can fully participate by speaking, listening, and thinking about what is being shared. Sitting in a circle is an important part of Word Problem Workshop too. The circle includes every student and signals that everyone is welcome and valued in our math discussion.

## 2) Thumbs Up

Have you ever felt the looming forest of raised arms growing around you as you speak? It feels as if the arms are flailing flags, signaling it's time to stop talking and move on to someone else. In the Discussion, we want students to feel empowered to share their ideas and feel like others listen to them when they do. We hope students see that sharing helps both them and their classmates understand the math, and that everyone deserves to be heard. That can't happen when hands are waving frantically in the air. Often, students eager to share their ideas become so focused on their own ideas that they stop listening to the speaker. Meanwhile, the raised hands are distracting the speaker from the idea they are trying to share.

Instead of raised hands, use thumbs up. When a student has an idea to share in the Discussion they simply put their thumb up on their knee (Figure D.4). This small change allows students to signal they have an idea ready to share without creating an intimidating thicket of raised arms.

## 3) Call on Each Other

In addition to the thumbs up signal, students can also take charge of calling on the next speaker during a discussion. After one student shares their idea,

**FIGURE D.4** A student raises their thumb to signal they have an idea to share.

they call on the next person to speak. I've found this simple change has three main benefits.

- **Benefit 1: Sense of pride.** Students find the task of calling on the next speaker to be a "big deal" and it boosts their feelings of ownership in the conversation. When I asked a third grader about calling on students in the Discussion he said, with a huge smile on his face, "We get to call on each other because we're in charge! Not the teacher, *us*!" He beamed with pride.

- **Benefit 2: Shifts the focus from the teacher to the students.** When students take charge of calling on each other, the teacher's voice fades to the background, allowing students to focus and pay attention to each other.

- **Benefit 3: Positions students to analyze and critique the reasoning of others.** When students have the opportunity to talk directly to one another rather than the conversation always feeding through the teacher, they become more focused on listening to understand and asking questions to better understand someone else's idea.

### *4) Cold Calls*

Cold calling on students means simply calling on any student, at any time. While this move can feel uncomfortable at first for students, when framed properly, cold calls can build engagement and investment from all students. This might sound like, "Remember friends, in this class every single one of us is thinking, even if we aren't sharing. We have to work together to make sure we all understand. Every idea, even if it is slightly off track, can help us move forward. We may call on you even if your thumb isn't up because we believe your ideas are valuable."

The class might moan and groan a bit. Reminding them that there is the option to take more time is important. "Remember, if you're called on and not quite ready to share that is okay, but we will come back to you. R'nyah, what might you say if someone calls on you and you need a minute?"

She looks at the chart (Figure D.5) and says, "I think I would say, 'Can you come back?'"

Rather than using cold calling to catch students off guard, frame it as an opportunity to include everyone's thoughts in the discussion. A fun challenge is to aim for 100% student participation in a conversation, with students working together to make sure everyone shares.

**FIGURE D.5** Giving students the language to momentarily opt out in a discussion helps boost students' willingness to participate overall.

### *5) The "What Did They Say?" Game*

The "What Did They Say?" game, also known as revoicing, is a simple but powerful tool. When a student shares an idea that you want others to hear and remember you can ask, "What did they say?" and have another student repeat the idea in their own words. Then point to a different student and say, "What did they say?" Repeat this process with several students. This repetitive game helps amplify important ideas, re-engage students, and check for understanding—all in one. This is the perfect game to use when you see students' attention start to drift.

### 6) Heads Together

Similar to a turn and talk, heads together is an opportunity for pairs of students to quickly share ideas. Often in the math discussion one person is talking while the others are listening. If these periods of time go on too long they can lead to disengagement. Heads together is a quick way to engage everyone. Students simply lean their heads toward each other and speak. Students don't even have to look at each other or move from their seat. Just simply leaning their head toward their partner and speaking can get everyone re-engaged. You can see this strategy in action at the 5:20 mark of this video from my classroom (follow the QR code).

## Facilitating Discussions for Deeper Understanding

Facilitating a Discussion during Word Problem Workshop is a balance between careful planning and on-the-spot improvisation. You'll use what you've observed during Grapple Time to guide the Discussion. Start with the ideas that students described in the Share. Then ask questions that help clarify and make connections between their ideas. Combine turn and talks, whole-group sharing, and questioning to help students stay engaged in the Discussion and continue to explore new ideas deeply.

During the Discussion you are the coordinator, the coach, and the caretaker. You will:

- Coordinate all the moving pieces and ideas, making sure to keep the Discussion on a productive path.

- Coach by asking questions that nudge students to think and discuss different aspects of the mathematics.

- Take care of each mathematician by encouraging participation, ensuring equity of voice, and upholding the norms.

Let's take a look at three of the most powerful teacher moves we can use when facilitating the Discussion. You can start with these moves right now and build on them for years to come.

## Listen

*LISTEN more* is something I wrote at the top of my Word Problem Workshop plans for years. I set this mantra for myself and took it seriously. I wanted to get good at facilitation, and I knew the only way to do that was to listen first instead of jumping in to explain. Putting my focus on listening allowed me to really figure out what my students knew. To do this during discussions, I would physically lean in toward the speaker and lock my eyes on them. I got on the floor to listen in during turn and talks (Figure D.6). I did this in part to model actively listening for my students, but these physical actions also helped remind me to truly get curious about what my students were saying and thinking.

In addition to making listening a priority for ourselves as teachers, we also need to support our students in learning how to actively listen. Take time to model how listening looks and sounds. Create an anchor chart like the one in Figure D.7 so you can refer back to those expectations before and during the Discussion.

**FIGURE D.6** Listening in to turn and talks is an important move to gain a deeper understanding of students' thinking.

## Question

Teachers often ask me for the perfect questions to use in a discussion. I can understand this request because I've spent hours as a teacher trying to write questions and test out which ones work best. And while I truly believe that there is no perfect question or set of questions, I do believe that good questions can help us gather more information, clarify students' ideas, prompt deeper thinking, and nudge students to make connections and generalizations.

Below are the questions I use most in the Discussion part of Word Problem Workshop. This is not an exhaustive list of the best questions to ask. I encourage you to try these as a starting point and add your own questions along the way.

**FIGURE D.7** An example of an Active Listening anchor chart from my third-grade classroom. We used this same chart across our day, in all subject areas, to help us remember and prioritize listening expectations.

- "What do you notice?"
- "What do you wonder?"
- "What is the same about the shares?"
- "What is different about the strategies and models shared?"
- "Which strategy is most efficient? Why?"
- "What does this represent?" (Here I am usually asking about what a number in a problem represents or what something in a student's work represents.)
- Repeating the question from the problem to refocus students on what they are trying to figure out.

## Notice Patterns in Your Questioning

Early in my teaching career I had a coach who would give me real-time feedback during math discussions. One day, she leaned in and whispered to me, "Mona, you're trying to get them to guess what's in your head." She noticed the back-and-forth pattern I was stuck in during which I asked increasingly leading questions to get students to say what I was thinking. We started to lovingly refer to this bad habit of mine as the "Guess What's In My Brain" game. Not only is this type of questioning unproductive for students' mathematical thinking, it also leads to disengagement.

Now when I facilitate a discussion, I focus on a more productive pattern that involves asking open-ended questions that encourage students to share and interact with one another's thinking. While I pre-plan questions and learning goals ahead of time, it's essential that the discussion flows from student thinking, not just answering my questions.

If you find yourself falling into an unproductive pattern of questioning, simply pause. Ask students to notice and wonder about a specific part of a strategy or student work. Then have them turn and talk. This pause gives you a moment to consider which open-ended question you might ask next. Being aware of our own questioning patterns (and changing course when we need to!) helps us grow as facilitators of math discussions.

## A Discussion Framework, Not a Recipe

While listening and asking questions are critical teacher facilitation moves in discussions, it's also important to understand the direction you want the discussion to take. After a decade of experimenting with different discussion frameworks, I developed one that effectively guides students from an open sharing of their ideas to deep mathematical understanding and forming a math conjecture (Figure D.8). This framework balances openness to student

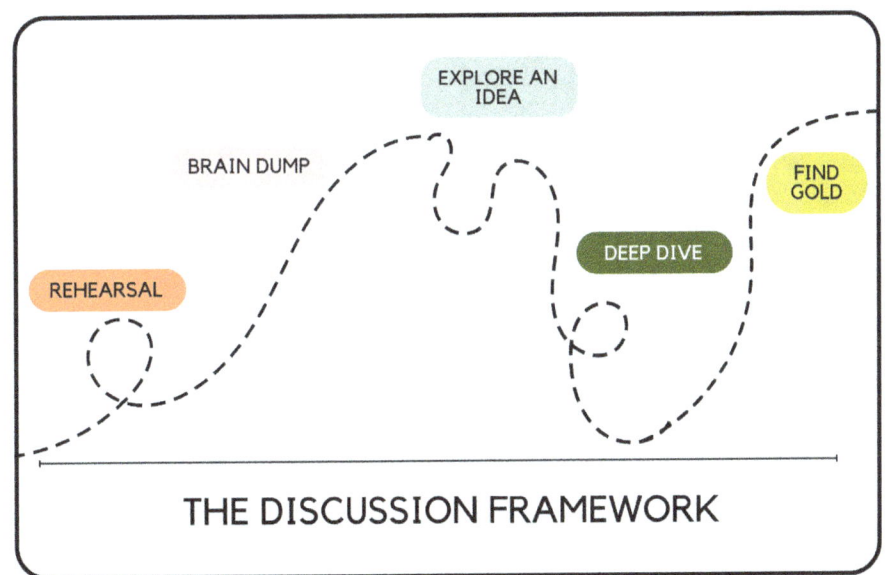

**FIGURE D.8** This illustration represents one way your discussion might flow.

thinking with the productivity needed to reach a meaningful conclusion. However, the Discussion Framework is just that, a flexible framework intended to help guide the Discussion flow, not a recipe or set of steps that must be rigidly followed.

Of course, not every discussion goes as planned, but this Discussion Framework is where I suggest everyone starts when implementing Word Problem Workshop. As you begin, just start with the first step and build up little by little until you are attempting the whole framework. Over time, you will adapt this framework as you strengthen your listening and questioning skills and refine your process. You might rearrange parts or skip sections based on the day, your students, or the problem at hand. Like building a campfire, leading a math discussion requires intuition and flexibility.

## *Rehearsal Time*

After the selected students have shared their ideas and work, encourage the rest of the class to notice and wonder about the strategies shared. Ask students to generate as many ideas as possible. For younger students this might sound like, "Use your slooooow turtle eyes to look at each step of Maria's strategy. What do you notice?" For older students, you might say, "Take a moment to notice and wonder about the strategies shared. Gather as many ideas as you can. Let your brain boil over with ideas as you notice each detail of their model."

Next give students time to rehearse before sharing in the whole-group discussion. Sharing ideas might feel like stepping out onto stage to perform a monologue to some students, so rehearsal is key. Ask students to turn and talk with a partner to share their thoughts and listen for new ideas. Even if a student doesn't have an idea to start, they can listen to their partner and leave the conversation with something new to share. By the time the whole-group discussion begins, every student has an idea, whether it's their own or something they've heard from their partner.

You'll find common prompts for rehearsal and other components of the framework in Figure D.9. Start by focusing on implementing rehearsal with your students. Practice this component consistently until your students build stamina for engaging in math discussions. This process will look different for every class, but it's essential to give students the time and space to develop their ability to discuss their math thinking. You don't need to implement all parts of the framework right away, but it's important to keep going and make progress each day.

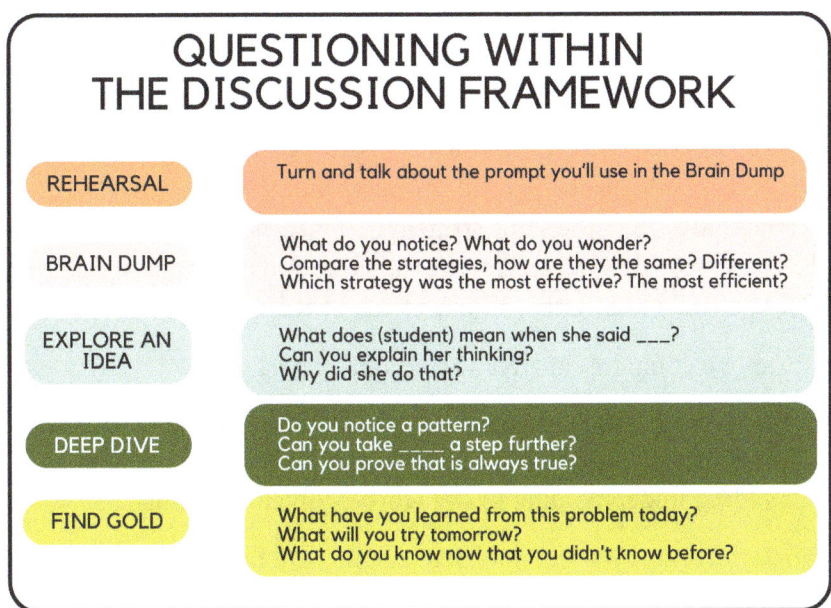

**FIGURE D.9** This quick reference sheet can support you in asking productive questions in each part of the Discussion Framework. Download a printable version at WordProblemWorkshop.com.

## *Brain Dump*

After a really fun day at Grammy's house my kids come home and excitedly share every detail, talking nonstop about everything they did, watched, tried, experimented with, tasted, and on and on. That's how I think of this time in the math discussion. We've built up anticipation from sharing, to silent notice and wonder, to a lively partner talk, and now it's time to share with the whole group to dump all the ideas out! This is a brain dump, a chance to get every idea out on the table so we can see what we're working with.

Launching this brain dump might sound like, "Okay. Let's hear all about what you're noticing up here. Jose, start us off. All eyes on Jose, active listening… Go ahead Jose!" Jose shares his ideas and calls on someone with their thumb on their knee. This process continues until ideas start to repeat or energy wanes. During this time, the teacher listens closely to assess students' understandings, spot misconceptions, and note when a student hits on the learning goal.

## *Explore an Idea*

Up to this point in the Discussion, we've relied solely on students' ideas to fuel the conversation—often without asking a single question. Now it is time to stoke the fire by offering a question that sparks discussion and brings it to a roaring flame. The goal of this part of the Discussion is to use a question to explore an idea brought up by students, and encourage everyone to think and talk more deeply about it. Ideally, this discussion aligns with your learning goal, but it may also explore a different important idea students have brought up.

For example, the teacher's language in this part of the Discussion might sound like, "Let's go back to what Megan said. She wondered why he added 10 and then 6. Who wants to talk more about that?" Or, "Many of you noticed the sharers had the same strategy. To me, they looked different. Can we talk about how these strategies are the same and how they are different?"

**Other possible questions you might ask at this point include:**

- Can we compare the first and second strategy?
- How does Tina's strategy show what is happening in the story? What in the story told her to do that? (This question supports building understanding of the word problem's language.)

Sometimes the brain dump reveals that students are far from the learning goal and aren't mentioning ideas close to it. In that case, nudge them forward by focusing on where they are in their understanding. For example, if your goal is for students to consider the efficiency of different strategies for addition, but the discussion shows students are stumped by a particular strategy, focus first on understanding the strategy shared before critiquing it for efficiency.

## Deep Dive

After exploring an idea (or a few), it's time to dig deeper into one. Typically, when exploring an idea you will start to notice students making connections, adding on to ideas, and kids using nonverbal signals to show their active engagement in the conversation. This is often when you'll ask a question related to why you chose the sharers' work that day in order to drive students' attention toward the learning goal. You will dive deeper into the ideas previously discussed and start making connections between the students' strategies on the board. This is often a time in the Discussion when the conversation sometimes stalls out. Once students notice, name, and all agree on the math, teachers can feel lost and may be left wondering, "Where do we go from here?"

Anchor this part of the Discussion to your learning goal, and push students to think critically. Use questions that prompt students to explain their reasoning and justify it with evidence. Noticing the sharers' steps to solve isn't enough—our students must unpack the *why* of those steps. A deeper dive ensures students leave the Discussion with solid, lasting understanding they can apply to future math problems.

You might consider asking one of these questions to prompt students to dive deeper and then turn and talk. With any turn and talk, but specifically during these ones, it is essential to listen in to student conversations. Listen with the purpose of finding a few students who can clearly explain their thinking. Then, when you bring the class back together you'll direct those students to share. This is one of the times you might take on the role of directing the conversation to the students you've heard are ready to share.

For example, I listened to a turn and talk in which Gabby and her partner, Beatrice, discussed why one student added and another subtracted but got the same answer. Gabby said, "Well it's like a fact family. You can subtract and add." Beatrice replied, "Yes, but I don't know how to prove it. She said we have to prove it."

Gabby confidently explained, "Well you have the total right, like the 37 and then the part that we didn't know was how many people left the playground. But we knew that 19 were still there. So, you can add the people that left with the people that were still there…" Beatrice interrupted, "But we don't know how many left."

"Right! So, that's why Omar subtracted. Because he knew the total, so he took away the 19 that were still there and that told him how many left." Gabby responded.

Hearing these two students discuss the quantities, and how the unknown's location changes with strategy, was encouraging. However, they were still working through their justifications. So, I told them we'd start the Discussion with their ideas.

I brought the class back together and said, "Eyes on Gabby. Gabby, can you explain what you and Beatrice were discussing about fact families?"

## Prompts to Dive Deeper

- Do you agree? Disagree?
- Explain why this works.
- Will this work every time? On other problems? Prove it.
- Can you prove this is always true?
- What properties of operations tell us this is true?
- Can we write a conjecture, something we think might be true in math, that we can apply and test out in future problems?
- Is this strategy effective?
- What makes this effective? Will it work every time?
- How could we improve the effectiveness or efficiency of this strategy?
- Would you use this strategy? Why or why not?
- Which of these strategies would you use next time? Why?

## Find Gold

As students engage in stronger and stronger discussions, they will often start to make generalizations about what they think might be mathematically true. In kid language, this might sound like a first grader saying, "You can add two numbers in any order and get the same thing," or a fifth grader saying, "When you multiply two whole numbers, usually they get bigger, but I am noticing that's not always true for decimals." Such discoveries, even if they seem simple to us as adults, can feel like striking gold for children. And it is gold! Thinking beyond computation toward generalizations and what might be mathematically true is important mathematical work across the grades. And it's important for children to know they're doing something really important when they make, test, and revise conjectures.

This "gold" may take many forms: explaining a property of a math operation, making a breakthrough in modeling or understanding why a strategy works. A math generalization or conjecture might align with your learning goal, but it often emerges from what resonates with students during the Discussion.

When listening in on these kinds of conversations in a classroom recently, students described conjectures as:

- "Something we think could be true and we can try in our next problems."
- "It's something you want to remember in the future."
- "A big part of what we talked about today, it could be something new we figured out."
- "You can check your work to make sure you've done those things."

Launching this part of the Discussion might sound like, "We've talked a lot today about fractions and these two different approaches to solve the problem. Is there a conjecture we can agree on?" After a turn and talk, students eagerly share. Jasper shares, "I think we can say that if the numerator is bigger than the denominator, you will have more than a whole." The teacher confirms consensus, invites students to add evidence, and records the generalization or conjecture at the bottom of the chart paper (Figure D.10). The students will build on these conjectures day after day, reminding each other of them during discussions by referring back to past conjectures and problems as they prove their mathematical reasoning in the Discussion.

You might have noticed that this student's conjecture represents an important understanding, but isn't *always* true (as in the case when the denominator is 0 and the numerator is > 0). The teacher notes this and will create opportunities for students to grapple with this idea in subsequent problems and revise their thinking. The act of returning to and revising conjectures is just as important as their initial creation.

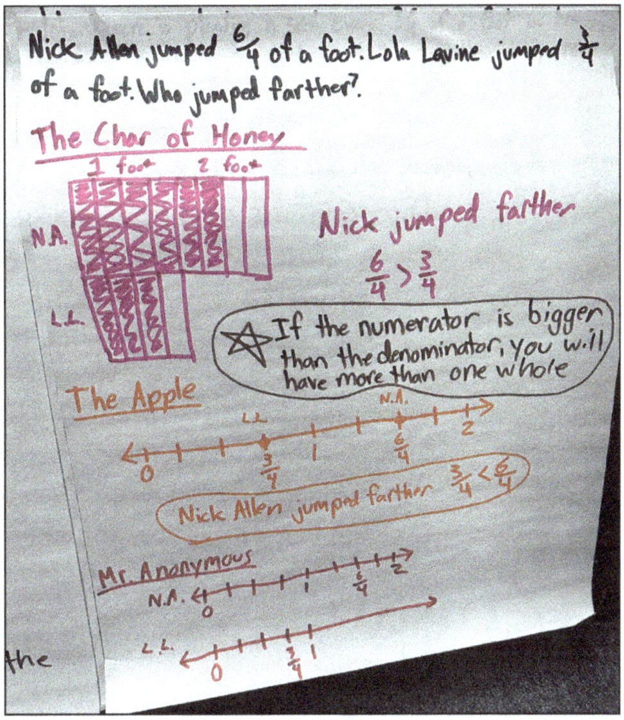

## Wrap Up or Trail Off...

Math discussions don't always end neatly, like a campfire that slowly flickers out as the group begins to wrap up for the night. Often, your discussion might end

**FIGURE D.10** A chart shows how students made a conjecture and the teacher recorded it on the Word Problem Workshop chart.

with, "Hmm… that's so interesting. Let's keep thinking about this and talk more about it tomorrow," leaving the door open for continued thinking. This invites students to see that making meaning is an ongoing process, extending beyond the math discussion.

Sometimes, however, your math discussion wraps up just right, like a campfire where the perfect amount of logs were added to keep it burning through the evening. It naturally concludes as the time around the fire comes to an end. In the previous fraction example, the teacher might wrap up the discussion by asking the class to continue thinking about the idea in the future. "We'll record Jasper's idea on chart paper here. I wonder if his idea that if the numerator is bigger than the denominator, you will have more than one whole is always true. We can keep coming back to this idea."

The best scenario is when every student leaves the math discussion feeling confident that they've understood what was discussed. As my former third-grade student, Maddie, put it, "It's our job to make sure everyone understands it [the math] each day." When students walk away from the Discussion knowing a bit more, feeling more confident to solve the next problem, or understanding another person's mathematical reasoning—it's a win.

# Common Questions from Teachers

## Should I Use Sentence Stems to Encourage My Students to Discuss?

Sentence stems are a valuable tool to help students get started in sharing their ideas. They can also serve to set expectations for the types of talk we want to hear in the Discussion. But not all uses of sentence frames in the classroom are created equal. In some cases, sentence frames can be more overwhelming than helpful to students. For example, some classrooms have a bulletin board labeled "Math Discussions" or "Accountable Talk" surrounded by a bunch of sentence stems. The board may be rarely used or referred to during the math discussion because it is far from the meeting space, making it hard to read. When there are a bunch of sentence stems on the board it takes students a lot of time to sort through which to use, pair it with their idea, and then hope to be called on while their comment is still relevant.

Alternatively, I suggest you use sentence stems more strategically. Select one or two stems you would like your students to focus on using that week or month. For example, you might include the sentence stems in Figure D.11 with the hope that students will compare and contrast the strategies shared and provide justifications for their assertions. Display the sentence stems right next to the Word Problem Workshop chart. Remind students at the start of each discussion that one of their goals is to try and use the sentence stem. This limits the amount of mental sorting students need to do and instead focuses their attention on using the language we hope to hear in the math discussion.

**FIGURE D.11** Two sentence frames you might offer students to encourage them to compare and contrast strategies.

## What if I Freeze During the Discussion and Don't Know What Question to Ask?

This is by far the most difficult part of facilitating a discussion. You'll find moments in which you're stumped and unsure of what to say next. With each passing moment the pressure builds because you're balancing wanting to get students to the intended learning goal, and also honoring their current thinking which may not be aligned to that goal. The best next move is to slow down, insert some time for students to talk in partners, and listen in to their thinking. Then, ask an open-ended question that will help you gain information on what they know and what they are not yet understanding or able to explain.

To help us think about this question further, let's consider this problem.

*The preschool classroom has two rugs pushed together in their gathering space. (See the diagram below.) What is the total area of the rugs?*

The goal of this lesson was to break a composite shape into smaller rectangles and find their area in order to calculate the total area.

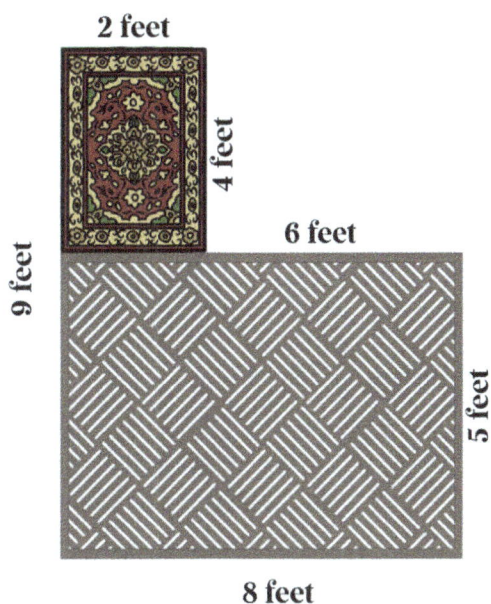

During the Discussion, the teacher, Jimmy, asked students to clarify their thinking and provided space and time for them to do so. He switched from the whole-group discussion to a turn and talk during a few key moments to gather his thoughts and allow students time to process what had been discussed. Then, about five minutes into the discussion, the students started to repeat the procedural steps for finding the area, "2 × 4 is 8 and 8 × 5 is 40 so the area is 48." Jimmy kept asking them less important questions about the units and was starting to get pulled into the messy game of "Guess What's In My Head?" He was stuck and unsure of how to proceed.

Jimmy decided to pull back and ask an open-ended question, "What is area?" The students were stumped, revealing the missing link in their understanding. They knew how to procedurally solve area problems, but could not yet explain the concept of area. This opened up an opportunity for Jimmy to ask more questions to nudge students' understanding of area using the problem's context of area rugs.

Students left the Discussion eager to tackle another problem and continue the conversation the next day. While there wasn't much closure, the Discussion sparked more questions. Now, Jimmy had a clearer sense of what students could do and knew which questions to ask to deepen their understanding the next day (and beyond).

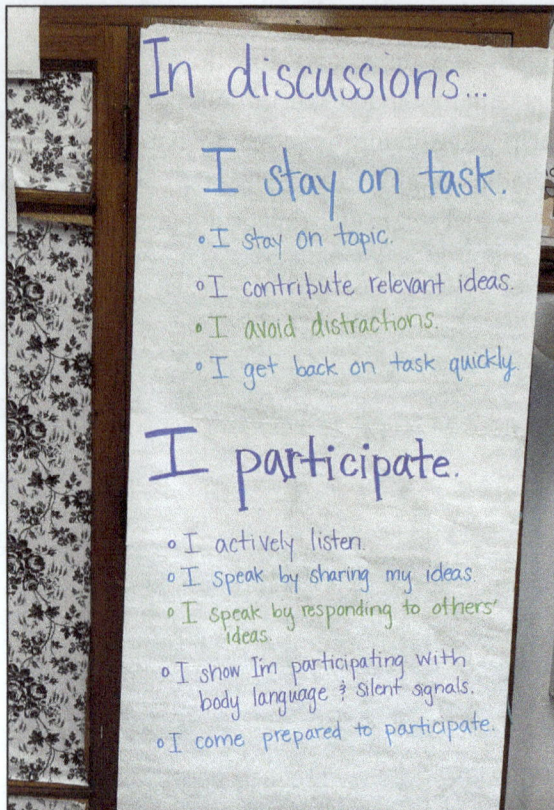

**FIGURE D.12** An anchor chart of expectations and norms can help students understand their role in the Discussion.

## What if My Students Won't Talk?

Get curious! Wondering why students are resistant to participating is helpful in planning for how you'll re-engage them. You might begin by asking them to write a reflection, look back at the math surveys you gave earlier in the year, or perhaps do another survey that targets questions around participation.

Next, you'll want to form some norms or ground rules for the Discussion (Figure D.12). These norms will help students see the safeguards in place to ensure they won't be made fun of for participating. This norm-forming conversation can also help students understand the purpose for math discussions. Often students think discussions are optional. Frame the "why" behind the Discussion. Make it clear that the Discussion is a big part of learning math and deepening their understanding beyond just finding answers.

## Be an Action Taker

### First Steps

- Circle students up for a math discussion, ensuring everyone can see each other and engage with one another.

- Switch from hand raising to thumbs up.

- Discussions thrive when students and teachers listen actively. Make the expectations for student listening explicit by creating a chart (Figures D.7 and D.12) and practicing those expectations. Then, during the next two weeks of discussion, model active listening yourself by prioritizing listening more than talking. Focus on understanding how students think about the problem and the ideas they share.

## Ready to Run

- Try building each piece of the Discussion Framework (Figure D.8). Implement the first part for a few days and then add on the next part. Remember, it is a framework, but not a recipe. The more you listen and tune into discussions, the better you will know what questions or moves need to come next to keep the Discussion productive and engaging.

- Reflect on engagement, once you're doing the "parts" of the Discussion it is time to dig in to see how you can make the most of the discussion time. Often that means engaging every student in listening, speaking, *and* thinking.

- Link your Discussion to your learning goal. Your questions and Discussion should build toward a deeper understanding of the learning goal. Utilize the quick question reference sheet in Figure D.9 to help you ask questions that deepen student understanding.

# Step 5: Reflect

After years of engaging students in grappling and discussing math word problems, I began to notice something unsettling. While my students could describe their reasoning and understand the strategies of their peers during discussions, they weren't always transferring that understanding to other problems. On tests or in their workbooks, students often reverted to the same strategies over and over again, often without showing any of the thought processes we had worked so hard to develop during Word Problem Workshop.

I started to question whether spending time sharing and discussing one problem was really worth it if my students weren't leaving Word Problem Workshop with something they could apply to future problems. It felt like the core of what I believed about teaching math—that productive struggle and discourse lead to deeper understanding—was crumbling.

Then it hit me. Students weren't making connections between Word Problem Workshop and the rest of math class because I hadn't given them the opportunity to reflect on their learning. As a longtime advocate for reflection as a powerful learning tool, I realized this was the missing link in our process.

This realization came into sharp focus when I was teaching my fifth graders about fractions. We spent several days exploring equal sharing fraction problems and then problems that required multiplying fractions. My students grappled with the problems, listened to their peers share strategies, and discussed the connections between those strategies and their own thinking. Students who initially struggled with fractions began participating and solving problems confidently. By the end of the week, I felt sure my students understood multiplying fractions.

But when I gave them a quiz, that confidence evaporated. Instead of showing their reasoning with a model or explaining their thinking, most students simply multiplied across the fractions to get an answer—relying on an age-old procedure—as though our discussions and explorations had never happened. I was, like many teachers, frustrated that no one was showing their work or showing what they had learned!

Then I had to confront the hard truth. Maybe they hadn't truly learned. Up until this point, I had not gathered any formative assessments, but expected everyone to breeze through the quiz. I also had given students no experience with synthesizing their problem-solving experiences and mobilizing their understanding to new problems. This humbling experience was the spark that nudged me to create the final step of Word Problem Workshop, Step 5: Reflect.

The day after the not-so-great fraction quiz, I introduced Reflection to my students after our Discussion. I shared two strategies for reflection: self-reflection and One More Problem. To reflect, I asked students to give a thumbs up, down, or in the middle in response to the statement, "I can explain my strategy." Students flashed their signal and I made note of students whose thumbs were down or in the middle. Next, I gave the students another problem to solve, similar to the one we had just discussed in Word Problem Workshop. I prompted them, "This is your chance to use your takeaways from today's Word Problem Workshop to try another problem. Show what you know and can do with this new problem."

Here are the problems I gave them:

**Word Problem Workshop Problem:** *There was $\frac{1}{2}$ of a pizza left. My brother ate $\frac{2}{3}$ of it. How much pizza is left for me?*

**One More Problem:** *There was $\frac{1}{3}$ of a pizza left. My brother ate $\frac{3}{4}$ of it. How much pizza is left for me?*

Reflecting on what they had learned and applying it to a new problem was transformative. Students connected their earlier explorations to their own understanding. For the first time, they demonstrated not just what they could do, but what they truly knew.

I've also learned that reflection isn't just about solving another problem. It's about processing feedback. During Word Problem Workshop, feedback comes in many forms: verbal and nonverbal cues during discussion; prompts; questions during Grapple Time; even grades on assessments. Teaching students to reflect on feedback prepares them to set goals and track their own progress.

Exploring and experiencing problem solving isn't enough on its own. Without reflection and an opportunity to apply their new ideas, students might not fully understand what they've learned. But when they take the time to reflect and practice new ideas, they unlock their own growth and begin to see themselves as capable, confident problem solvers.

> **We can** provide students with opportunities to reflect, helping them consolidate their learning and apply their understanding to future problems. When students take the lead setting goals and taking action, they become invested decision makers in their mathematical journeys.

## Reflection Is Vital to Learning

Reflection is not the part of the Word Problem Workshop you skip when you run out of time. In fact, I would argue that Reflection is the most important part! This step provides you, the teacher, with the information you need to assess if students are making progress in their understanding. Reflection allows you to understand what students can do now that they couldn't do at the start of math class or at the start of the unit. Reflection also gives you the perfect opportunity to give students feedback and provide time for them to set goals for improvement. Although this time is flexible, I urge you to always reserve five minutes at the end of Word Problem Workshop to do some sort of reflection to help synthesize and solidify students' learning.

This chapter will focus on how to help our students reflect on their learning, apply what they have learned, and use feedback to deepen their understanding. We will also dive into the role of assessment and gathering data at the end of Word Problem Workshop. As we enter into the Reflection step let's center our focus on reflecting on both the academic skills gained and the human skills our students develop during this problem-solving experience.

### Goals of the Reflection

- Synthesize learning to consolidate understanding
- Apply or revise math work based on new insights
- Give and respond to meaningful feedback
- Empower students to identify next steps in their learning journey

## Reflect to Synthesize Learning

At the end of Word Problem Workshop it is essential that we help students bridge the gap between that day's problem-solving experience and future problems they will encounter. We want students to synthesize their learning and be ready to apply their new understandings in the future. Three reflection activities are particularly helpful for synthesizing learning.

1. One More Problem
2. Revise your work
3. Prove a conjecture

### *One More Problem*

One More Problem is a reflection routine in which you offer students a similar word problem to the one they solved in Word Problem Workshop as an opportunity to independently try out or apply what they learned. Trying this kind of reflection with students might sound like, "We've just discussed two different strategies for this equal sharing problem. Now I'm going to give you a new, but similar problem to try on your own. Think about how you might try a new strategy or revise the strategy you used on the first problem." The One More Problem reflection strategy is a natural formative assessment. You can use students' work to check in on individuals' progress, give feedback, or to plan for the next Word Problem Workshop.

One More Problem is:

- The same problem type as the previous problem students solved in Word Problem Workshop
- The same level of complexity (in numbers and context) as the previous problem
- Limited to a short time for solving (similar to Grapple Time)

- Framed as "an opportunity to show what you've learned"
- Used to gather information about students' progress and give feedback to students

### In Action: One More Problem

One afternoon a class of third-grade students has just solved this problem:

*Professor Sprout has 2 bookcases in her office that hold her herbology texts. Each bookcase has 4 shelves. One bookcase has 9 books on each shelf and the other has 12 on each shelf. How many herbology books does Professor Sprout have on her shelves?*

Some of the students in the classroom struggled to find a strategy that worked, while others used visual models to show their strategies and make sense of the problem. The teacher chose three students to share their strategies, including two that drew the bookcases (the purple and red strategies in Figure R.1). During the Discussion students focused on making sense of the problem and relating it to these models. Finally, the Discussion turned to the green strategy (Figure R.1). Students noticed that this sharer did not draw the bookcases but rather modeled the quantities by putting the number of books on each shelf in circles and adding these numbers up in a similar way to the other two sharers. Students spent time in

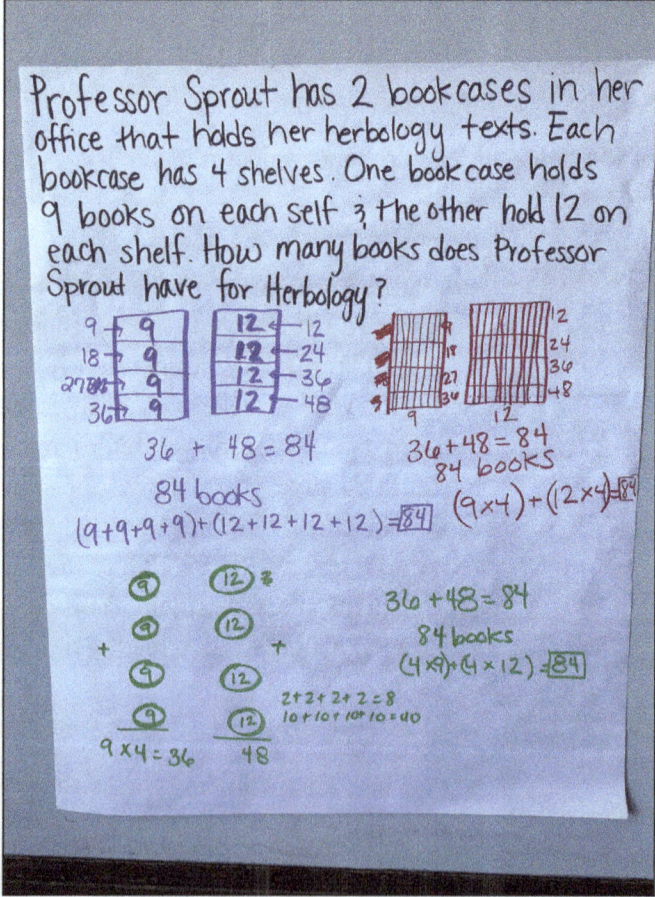

**FIGURE R.1** Students solved this problem in Word Problem Workshop prior to getting One More Problem to show what they learned from the Discussion.

the Discussion comparing the sharers' different equations and making connections between repeated addition and multiplication. This multi-step problem also gave students an opportunity to discuss how to represent multiple steps in a single equation.

As the Discussion wrapped up, the teacher asked students to do another problem that she called an exit ticket (Figure R.2). This "One More Problem" was also about bookcases in a professor's office, keeping the context of the problem consistent. The teacher drew the model on the board and asked students to write a number sentence to match the new problem and find the total number of books. This was a strategic choice to link One More Problem to the focus of the Discussion. Students were able to solve this additional problem quickly, as time was limited, but still try out some new thinking from the Discussion.

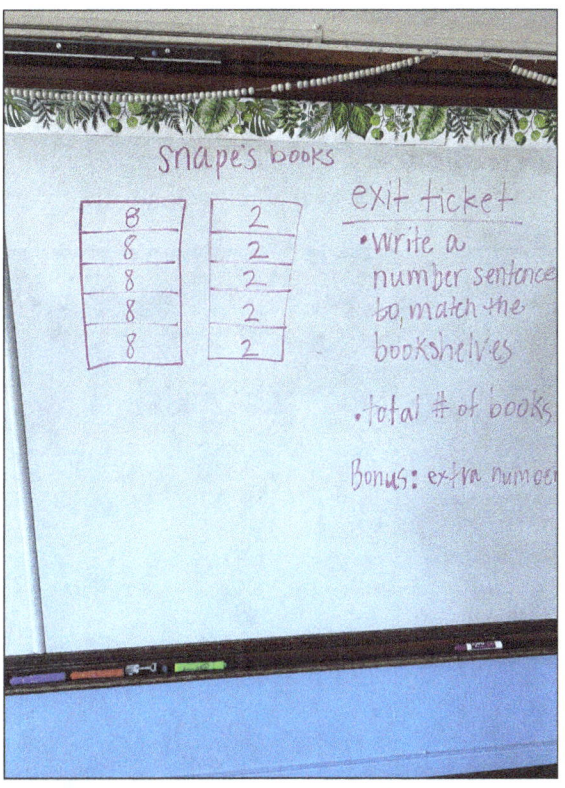

**FIGURE R.2** This exit ticket gives students One More Problem with different numbers but a consistent context to the main problem of Word Problem Workshop.

## Revise Your Work

Another way to use reflection time is to give students time to revise their work. After students have discussed the strategies shared they sometimes notice a mistake they made and want to fix it. Other times students have new ideas for making their work more efficient or accurate. Providing time for students to revise allows them to reflect on what worked and what didn't, and then to take action accordingly. Revising work is a great option when time is limited at the end of Word Problem Workshop. By giving students just two minutes to revise their work you're able to help students bridge the gap between what they did before and what they can do now.

## Prove a Conjecture

At the end of the Discussion part of Word Problem Workshop the class may have come up with a conjecture. Reflection time can be used to allow students time to test or prove the conjecture. For example, during a Discussion, one class made the conjecture: "When you cut a cake into more pieces they get smaller. So, $\frac{1}{6}$ is smaller than $\frac{1}{2}$." During the Reflection students had the opportunity to go back to their seats with materials to prove that this conjecture was, in fact, true. Some students, working in small groups or partnerships, partitioned Post-It notes or used fraction tiles to justify their reasoning. Then, as Reflection time came to a close, the teacher asked students to take a quick gallery walk to view other students' work and ideas. Finally, students gathered for a quick wrap-up discussion to come to consensus around their conjecture.

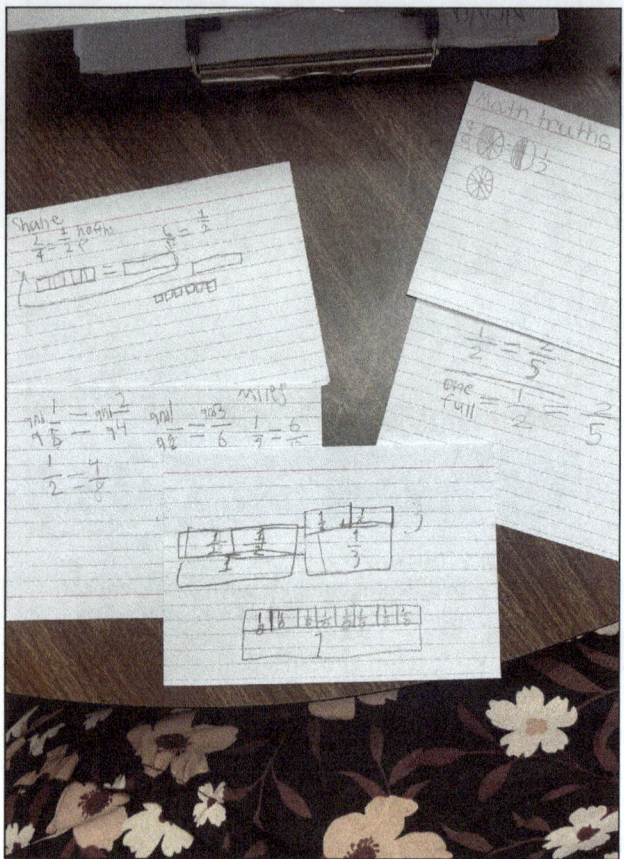

**FIGURE R.3** Students work to prove a conjecture on index cards, making it easy for the teacher to collect and review their responses.

Providing time for students to prove a math truth is a great way to reflect on the learning that occurred during Word Problem Workshop (Figure R.3). However, this reflection strategy often takes more than just a few minutes. If time is limited, you can postpone this reflection to the following day prior to starting a new Word Problem Workshop. You might give students time to prove a conjecture once or twice a month as your students develop key mathematical conceptual understanding.

## Self-Reflection

The Word Problem Workshop classroom is a space that engages students in exploring and sharing their current ideas while also developing new ideas. The daily Word Problem Workshop routine prepares our students for a life of learning through problem solving. In order to achieve that goal, our students must master more than just math standards. The University of Chicago's Consortium on School Research has carefully examined the field's key findings and amassed solid evidence that noncognitive factors are strongly linked to academic performance, which in turn predicts positive life outcomes. They argue that "fostering noncognitive factors that standardized tests don't measure: the behaviors, attitudes, beliefs, and social-emotional skills set students up for success in school and in life" (The University of Chicago Consortium on School Research 2017, 2). Embedding reflection on both academic and social ideas into Word Problem Workshop helps students develop lasting learning and skills.

Self-reflection is considering your thoughts, actions, and experiences in order to gain a deeper understanding, improve decision making, and guide future behavior. Self-reflection helps students learn from their successes and mistakes, promoting growth mindset and self-awareness. Self-reflection in Word Problem Workshop can be a quick thought prompt and hand signal, or a longer opportunity to think and write.

## Self-Reflect on the Habits of a Mathematician

It is helpful for students to reflect on their mathematician habits—the behaviors, attitudes, beliefs, and social-emotional skills that shape their identities as mathematical thinkers. Creating a class definition of who a mathematician is and their habits is useful as students start to reflect. The chart in Figure R.4 shows a list of descriptions and skills that one class built on throughout the year. The teacher used this list as a jumping-off spot for creating mini lessons and experiences designed to help students think more about these mathematician habits throughout the year.

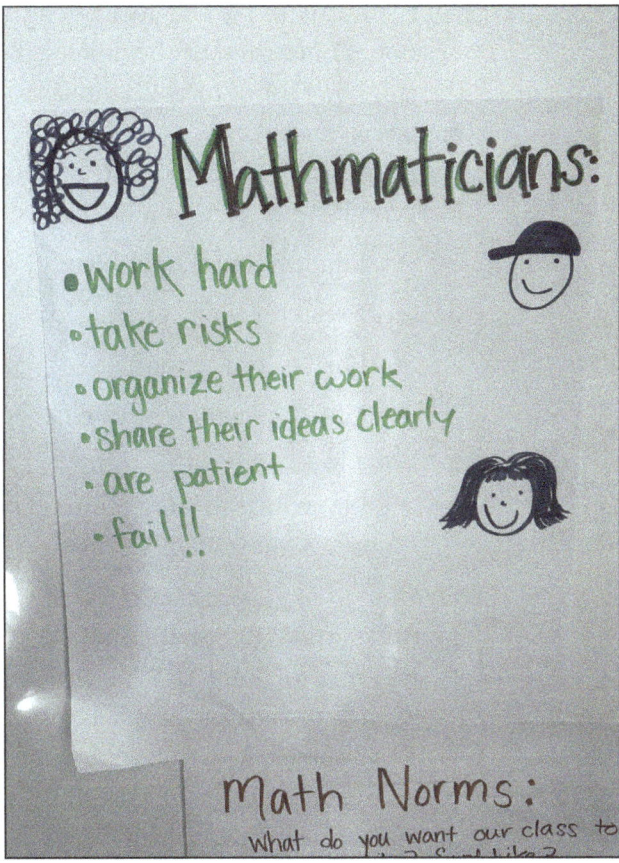

**FIGURE R.4** A chart one class brainstormed about the habits of mathematicians.

### In Action: Self-Reflection

Ms. Fess calls her students over to the carpet to examine several students' Word Problem Workshop notebooks in the center of the circle. Prior to the self-reflection she asked five students if the class could look at their notebooks. She pointed students' attention to a new descriptor on their Habits of a Mathematician chart: "I keep my work organized." Then, in groups of three, her students flip through the notebooks and discuss what it means to be organized, and why a mathematician, in particular, would need to be organized. Students point out examples from the notebooks such as how students used every page, dated their pages, and wrote their equations in the same spot on each page. They notice that this organization makes the work easier to understand. Ms. Fess records a few action steps that everyone in the class agrees to try out, including keeping their math notebooks organized and making their work clear.

You can create a list of mathematician habits by brainstorming with your students as well as identifying qualities you hope your students will develop as mathematical thinkers. Below is a list of qualities to get you started. For a list of forty qualities, one for each week of the school year, see the online resources.

**A list of mathematician qualities to engage students with during Reflection:**

- I understand the problem.
- I keep my work organized.
- I make connections.
- I don't give up when I face a challenge.
- I'm willing to start again when I get stuck.

Once your class has established a starting list of mathematician habits, it's time to begin reflecting on them. Reflections can be quick or more in depth, but they follow the same three-step process. Figure R.5 outlines these steps, which work for both Quick Checks and deeper reflections.

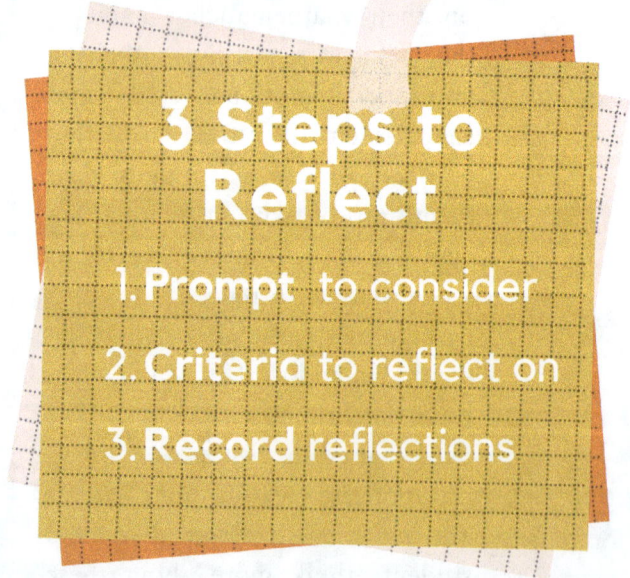

**FIGURE R.5** The 3 Steps to Reflect are used for Quick Checks and Deep Reflections. This simple three-step process helps students know what to expect during a reflection.

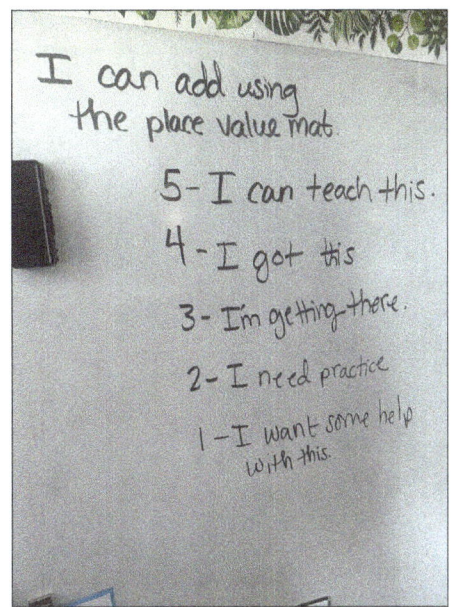

**FIGURE R.6** Writing the self-reflection criteria on the board can help students consider how they're doing.

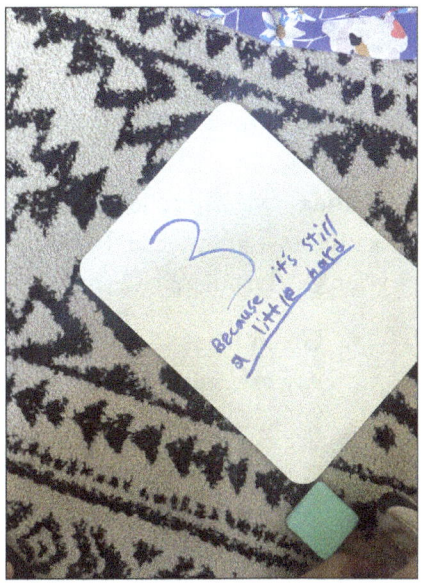

**FIGURE R.7** Whiteboards also can be used to record students' Quick Check reflections. This student chose to write words along with the number.

The self-reflection process begins by providing a prompt connected to a mathematician habit. Then, make the reflection concrete with clear criteria. For example, you might say, "Today, we're reflecting on staying focused the whole time to solve the problem. Rate yourself a 3 if you stayed focused the entire time, a 2 if you were somewhat distracted but worked for most of the time, and a 1 if you struggled to stay focused or didn't use your time for solving." Share the criteria verbally to help students more fully understand the goals (Figure R.6). Providing examples from what you observed during Word Problem Workshop also helps students reflect honestly and accurately. Finally, have students share their reflections with you, either by writing them down (Figure R.7) or giving a simple signal.

## Quick Checks

When time is very limited, use this reflection strategy that will take just a minute. Quick Checks are different because they do not ask students to explain or provide evidence, but instead simply to give a signal or number. The prompt and criteria are followed by a quick reflection period and an opportunity for students to record their reflection. Often the reflection is a hand signal or turning their paper into a bin that indicates their reflection.

### In Action: Quick Checks

To launch a Quick Check reflection, a teacher might say:

"Today we will reflect on our weekly mathematician habit—confidence. How confident do you feel in your work today? Use three levels today:

- Green means *I am confident with my strategy and answer. I am confident I understand the problem.*
- Orange means *I am confident with some parts, but other parts I'm still confused or not sure about.*
- Pink means *I am not confident because I'm still confused and I need more time with this problem and other problems like it so that I can be confident.*

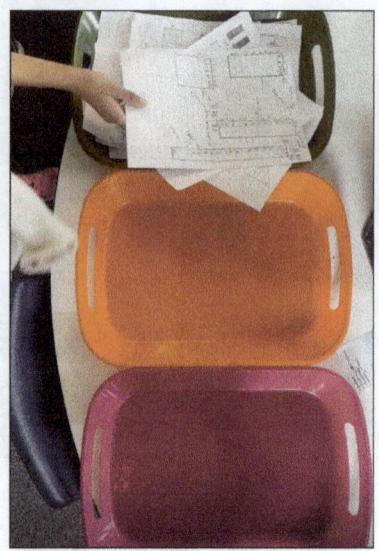

**FIGURE R.8** Colored trays are one way to help students record their reflection.

Take a few seconds to reflect on how you're feeling. When you're ready, place your paper into the colored tray (Figure R.8) to record your reflection."

Alternatively, you could easily change the criteria and substitute hand signals (thumbs up/to the side/down or numbers on their fingers) instead of the colored trays.

The prompt and criteria can also be printed on students' work. Then, at reflection time you can direct students' attention to that portion of their worksheet and ask them to mark their reflection. Figure R.9 shows how I added the mathematician behavior and criteria on students' papers. Then, they simply circled 4, 3, 2, 1 to record their reflection.

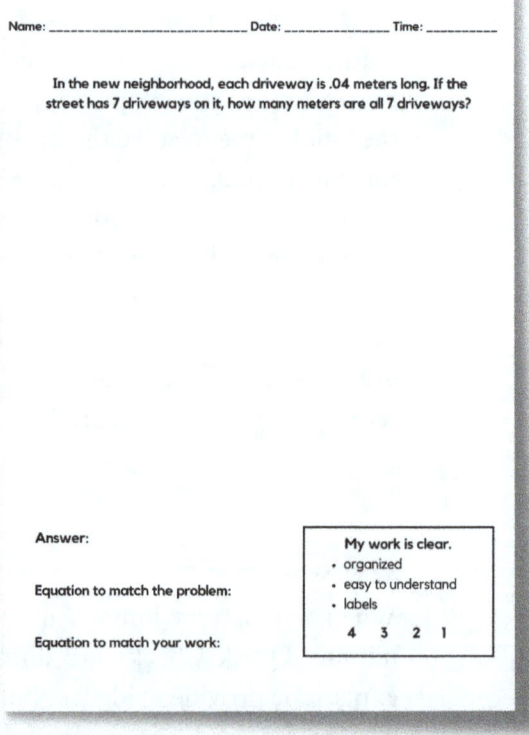

**FIGURE R.9** Example of a math goal setting worksheet.

144   Word Problem Workshop

**Quick Check Reflections**

- Thumbs up/Thumbs down
- Fingers showing a number
- Colored trays
- Whiteboards

## Deep Reflections

Longer reflections allow students to elaborate on their thoughts and provide more detail (compared to Quick Checks during which students might just provide a number or a hand signal as their reflection). Use Deep Reflections when introducing a new mathematician habit or helping students notice their progress. Limit these to about five minutes, once every week or two, to gain valuable insight into students' thinking. Deep Reflections can help you plan future lessons and interventions to support the development of mathematician habits and skills.

### In Action: Deep Reflections

To launch a Deep Reflection the teacher might give the prompt such as, "I took a risk today." Then, to clarify the criteria on which to reflect, they might say, "Think about how you grappled today and how you participated in the Discussion. Did you take any risks? Did you do anything that you weren't sure would work out? Take a moment to think."

Students sit for thirty seconds and then the teacher might add a few more thought joggers, "Maybe you had to push yourself to try a new strategy or you said something that felt risky. For some people, this might look like sharing an idea with the group or disagreeing with a friend during turn and talk. Risks are different for everyone. What feels risky to me might feel easy to you, and that's okay. In just a moment you'll get a chance to write about your risk taking today. Push yourself to write about a risk you took. If you can't think of one, then you can reflect on why you didn't take a risk. What might you need in the future to take more risks in math? We will take three minutes to get some ideas on our paper and then check in."

As the teacher gives directions she places an index card on each student's desk and sets the timer for three minutes. After three minutes she asks students to put up a finger for how many minutes they still need, "Show me with your fingers do you need zero, one, or two more minutes to finish?" Students show the signals and she decides, "One more minute. If you're finished, reread what you wrote and try to add a detail. Once the minute is up you'll put your card in a pile in the middle of the table to be collected and then take out your social studies notebook."

**Ways to Record Deep Reflections**

- In a partner conversation
- On an index card
- On the back of their work
- In a math journal or reflection form

## *Reflect to Goal Set*

Quick Checks and Deep Reflections often uncover students' areas for improvement. Setting and working toward goals helps students take ownership of their learning and stay invested in their progress. The goal of reflections is to help students identify areas for improvement and create a plan for progress. Ideally, students set goals and track progress throughout a unit, with daily reflections in between these larger goal-setting moments.

## In Action: Goal Setting

Goal setting in the classroom might be prompted by returning graded work and asking students to set a goal for their learning. The teacher might say, "Take a look at yesterday's word problem that I just returned to you. I've given you some feedback. Look at the circled parts. Think about what the feedback is telling you. What do you understand? What do you need more work on? What do you want to do going forward?"

Then the teacher gives students a few minutes to complete a goal-setting sheet like the one in Figure R.10. "Write down one thing you want to work on improving as you work on word problems this week. Then, select two or three ways you can do that from the list below. We will come back to this sheet each day so you can track your progress."

Giving students time to reflect on written work before setting a goal helps students set a goal based on evidence from their work. The teacher provides a minute each day for students to return to their goal and consider how they did. "If, for most of math time today, you work toward or accomplished your goal, put a 4 in Day 1's box. If your goal is to participate during the Discussion and you spoke up today, you might give yourself a 3 or 4 in the box. However, if you didn't speak today you might put a 1. Remember, you will have another chance to work on your goal tomorrow."

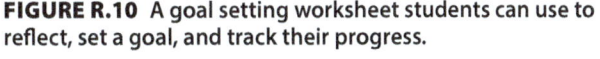

**FIGURE R.10** A goal setting worksheet students can use to reflect, set a goal, and track their progress.

## Reflect on Feedback

An important part of reflection is learning to accept and use feedback. For students who have little experience receiving feedback, it might feel like an uncomfortable or negative experience to them at first. We can work to change this by framing feedback as simply information that can help students improve. Figure R.11 shows an anchor chart which I created with my class in order to help them better understand feedback. We referred back to this chart often before reviewing feedback or graded work.

Feedback is most powerful when the message is specific and helpful. Effective feedback can take many forms in Word Problem Workshop including: quick verbal reminders, conferring nudges, circling parts of the

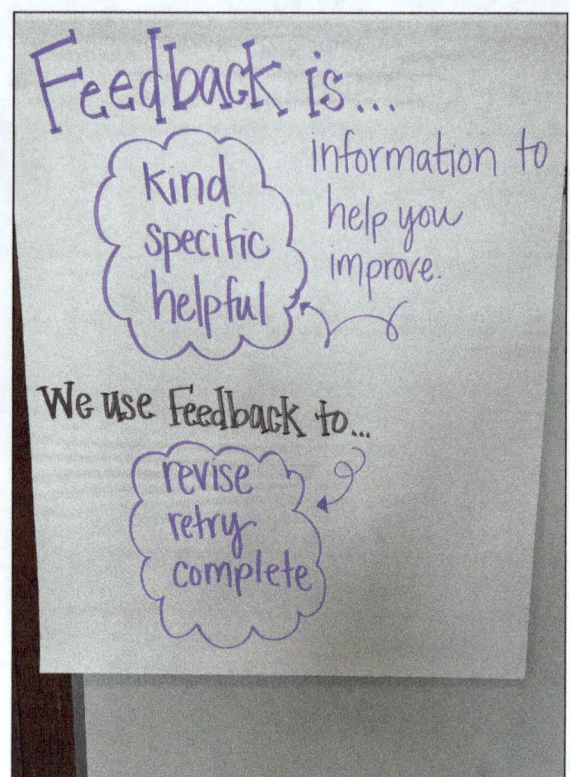

**FIGURE R.11** An anchor chart that defines an important concept like feedback can serve as a visual reminder to students. This is my class's feedback anchor chart that we referred to when getting and giving feedback.

students' work for them to revise, leaving written comments on students' work, assigning grades, or providing students with a checklist of success criteria.

## Checklist for Feedback in Word Problem Workshop

A checklist is an effective way to give students feedback on their Word Problem Workshop work. The checklist I share in this section is specifically for providing feedback on students' written work.

Before giving students feedback with a checklist, it is important that students know what each bullet point means. Spend time breaking down each criteria on the checklist to ensure students understand the expectations. Make sure to include a sufficient number of criteria on your checklist to motivate your students to do excellent work, but not so many as to overwhelm them. Younger students might start with just one point on the checklist and add on to the list as the school year goes on and they are ready to take on more challenges.

There are opportunities to give students feedback on each step of Word Problem Workshop. For example in the Grapple chapter we discussed a checklist for Clarity, Accuracy, and Precision. That checklist is very helpful when giving students feedback. I encourage you to create checklists that encompass the behaviors and expectations for the specific part of Word Problem Workshop and give students feedback to help them improve.

Checklist feedback is easy to give and clear for the student—that's a win-win! Print multiple copies of the checklist to have on hand and simply staple to the student's work (Figure R.12). Or, if your students are using a notebook for Word Problem Workshop, you can glue the checklist onto the page of their notebook.

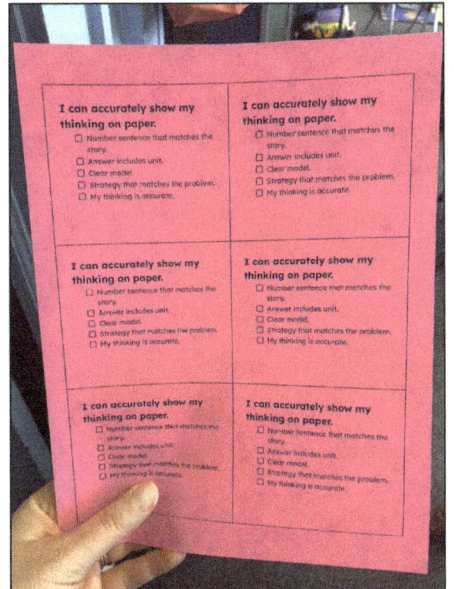
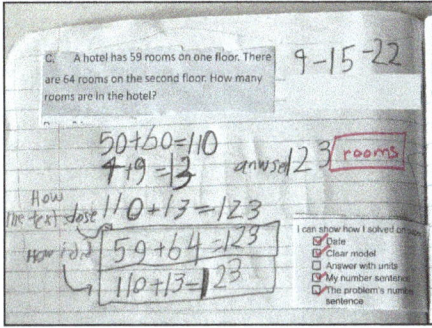

**FIGURE R.12** Putting multiple copies of the checklist on one page makes it easy to print (and saves paper!) (left). Then checklists can be easily glued into students' notebooks to give feedback (right).

As with many new structures and processes, creating a routine to unpack and use feedback will help students know what to expect and get the most out of the feedback. The first several times you give students feedback, you will need to help them understand and respond to the written feedback. Below is a sample routine for helping students unpack teacher feedback on their work.

**Unpacking Feedback:**

- Give student the work and marked checklist
- Student looks at the feedback and reflects (thinks!)
- Give students a prompt to consider (i.e., What went well? What parts are you still working on? Is there anything you need to ask for help with?)
- Ask students to record their ideas, make revisions, or set a goal in response to the prompt

## Reflect to Plan the Next Problem

Once you have reached the end of Word Problem Workshop for the day you should set aside some time for your own reflection. Consider what you learned about your students as mathematicians. Notice the trends in

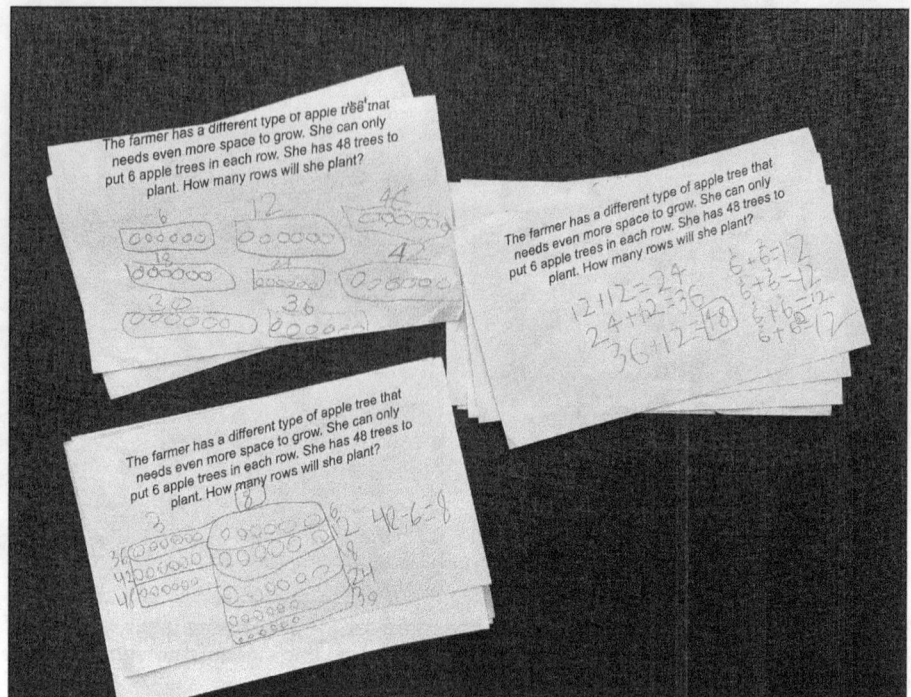

**FIGURE R.13** One way to sort student work is by the different strategies students use to solve a problem.

students' understanding and how they are changing day after day. Knowing where your students are on the trajectory of learning mathematics is important to helping you plan to support and challenge students.

One way to quickly reflect on students' work is to sort it (Figure R.13). Briefly examine each student's One More Problem. Then, sort them into one of three piles: "Got it," "Didn't get it," "Somewhere in between." These are intentionally broad categories because the specifics will vary based on the problem, learning goal, and your students. However, spending just five minutes sorting your students' work will help you notice trends and consider next steps. These trends can inform the problems you choose for the next day or week. For example, you may notice that nearly every student is leaving the "equation to match the problem" space blank on their paper. This noticing might lead you to choose problem types and a learning goal for the following week that will help students focus on writing equations that match the problem.

As my colleague Mark said, "The whole Word Problem Workshop is formative assessment. It informs the next Word Problem Workshop. The discussion from today helps me decide if students need a more challenging problem tomorrow. When all the students can discuss easily and are bored it is time to up the rigor. Then, I look at their work more closely and I can see exactly what I need to level up."

The idea that the entire time you're facilitating Word Problem Workshop you are also formatively assessing is really exciting, right? You don't need an exit ticket per se, but instead you can watch and listen to how students are discussing the problem and the strategies they use to assess their thinking. As you reflect on your observations you might consider:

- Can everyone describe the learning goal in their own words?
- Are students clearly communicating their reasoning (orally and on paper)?
- Can students justify their reasoning? Not just show what they did and why, but explain why it works.

## Common Questions from Teachers

### What if I Don't Have Time for Students to Reflect with One More Problem?

As you are getting started with Word Problem Workshop you probably will run out of time. Don't let the timing discourage you or cause you to give up. The more you facilitate Word Problem Workshop the better you will get at pacing. In the beginning, focus on making sure students understand the problem and are building confidence in grappling with the problems. Next, focus on using the Discussion time effectively to deepen students' understanding. This is not to say the Reflection is least important (I actually think the contrary) but rather that it can be the last part to focus on when you're first getting started. Build up to the Reflection. For more on what to focus on and when, check out the "Getting Started Guide" in the online resources.

If you do run out of time, you can do a simple Quick Check on a mathematician's habit or just a minute or two of revising work. As an elementary teacher you might be self-contained, teaching your students all day, which allows you some flexibility. If you have to end Word Problem Workshop to go to Spanish class, then when you return to the classroom, you might ask students to spend three minutes solving another problem. Alternatively, you can start the next day's math class with a quick reflection about the mathematician's habit to set a focus for that day's Word Problem Workshop.

## What if My Students Are Resistant to Reflection?

It is common for students to be uncomfortable or inexperienced with honest reflection. Some students feel like they might get in trouble for telling the truth about unfavorable behaviors like not trying or being off task. When you provide space for honest reflections students will see that being truthful and thoughtful in their reflection is the first step in growing and learning.

Modeling with a think aloud can be a powerful way to encourage the kind of reflection you're hoping that students will learn to do. For example, you might say something like, "Sometimes when I'm thinking about what I did, I get embarrassed because it wasn't my best work. I don't really want to admit I'm a 1 at this skill, but if I lie I might not get the feedback or help I need. It's a risk to say, 'I'm a 1 because I don't understand.' One time when I was a fourth grader I..." By sharing a vulnerable moment from your own experience, you provide students with a mental model for self-reflection.

Building the skills to reflect takes time. Don't give up because students are struggling. Instead, you can view their one- or two-word answers as an opportunity to teach them how to reflect. Continue giving students opportunities to practice this skill. Open up a discussion with students about what makes a good reflection. Create a criteria list and then give feedback on the quality of their reflections.

## Be an Action Taker

### First Steps

- Commit to two minutes of Reflection after Word Problem Workshop for the next few weeks.

- Do a Quick Check at the end of Word Problem Workshop using thumbs or finger numbers.

- Give students One More Problem. Keep the story the same, just switch up the numbers. Then collect students' work and see how they did.

## Ready to Run

- Create a checklist to give your students feedback on their work. Keep it simple at first. Get into the habit of giving feedback and helping students use it to improve.

- Decide on a mathematician habit to focus on for the month. Start by creating a chart that you can add to each month. Throughout the month, intentionally highlight and reinforce the chosen habit during math discussions and throughout the school day.

- Plan two days when students will do a Deep Reflection (5–7 minutes) on the monthly habit.

# Planning for Word Problem Workshop

Mark, a third-grade teacher colleague, and I sit down during our prep period, him on the bench next to the window and me at my desk next to him. "Let's plan math!" he says as he opens his laptop. In this single prep Mark and I aim to plan a week of Word Problem Workshop in which students will explore, problem solve, face some challenges, and, with some productive struggle, ultimately come away with a stronger understanding of the math we are studying. We have a lot of work ahead to accomplish this in a single prep period, and between Mark's jokes and reality TV updates, we'll need to stay focused!

We pull up the district's scope and sequence and our curriculum unit guide. The next unit for our third graders is adding and subtracting within

1,000. The curriculum marches students through a boot camp of strategies day after day. Each lesson teaches a strategy and asks students to independently practice only that strategy as they solve problems on their worksheets. Mark and I take note of these strategies so we can be sure our students have opportunities to use and analyze each one, but we're going to go about teaching this unit in a different way.

Instead of starting each lesson by showing students how to solve a problem and then asking them to mimic the steps we modeled, we will follow the five steps of Word Problem Workshop. We know that all of our students come to our classrooms with rich experiences and knowledge from which to draw. They are problem solvers at home, in their neighborhoods, and in other subject areas. They also have experiences and strategies for adding and subtracting smaller numbers that they can bring to and extend upon in this unit. With this in mind, we will start from what we know our students can do and build from there.

Mark and I pull up the standards for the unit and begin to unpack and make sense of them. Even though Mark and I have studied these standards in depth in past years as well, we know it is always important to return to the standards to ensure we know what skills and understandings our students should achieve by the end of the unit or year. After our brief standard unpacking conversation Mark and I determine the most important skills our students should be able to do by the end of our unit:

1. Solve two-step word problems with addition and subtraction
2. Write an equation that matches the problem with the unknown quantity represented as a letter or mystery box
3. Justify the reasonableness of answers by using estimation
4. Fluently add and subtract within 1,000 using algorithms ("naked numbers" as well, not word problems only)
5. Use algorithms that are based on place value, properties of the operations, and the relationship between addition and subtraction

We briefly discuss our students' current skills and understanding with these standards. Most of our students met or exceeded the math benchmark on a recent standardized test, but lack experience with problem solving and rely heavily on memorized procedures. While most can solve addition and subtraction problems with two- and three-digit numbers using the standard algorithm, they struggle to explain their reasoning. Most students have few alternative strategies for addition and subtraction problems, but do show strong number sense and base-ten understanding in other contexts.

Mark and I are now ready to choose problems to match our goals. Before we write our own problems, we look through the ones presented in our curriculum resources. We find the first word problem at the end of Lesson One's problem set.

> *Dad counted 800 flowers in his garden. 43 of the flowers are pink and the rest are white. How many white flowers are in Dad's garden?*

We choose this problem because it offers a good balance of being a familiar problem type (Part-Part-Whole, Part Unknown), while also challenging students to think about regrouping when subtracting. In fact, these numbers may encourage students to add up (43 + 7 = 50, 50 + 50 = 100, 100 + 700 = 800, 7 + 50 + 700 = 757 white flowers) instead of subtracting, subtract off in parts (800 – 40 = 760, 760 – 3 = 757 white flowers), or compensate (800 – 50 = 750, 750 + 7 = 757 white flowers) to make the subtraction more efficient.

A moment after selecting this problem, Mark rethinks the decision. "Honestly, I think this might be too easy for most of my kids. Should we make it a multi-step problem to up the rigor?"

"You love the word 'rigor,'" I say "Yeah, I agree. The kids can solve these kinds of problems, let's add in another step. Let's draft a new problem in our plan." Mark drafts this revised problem in our plans.

> *Dad counted 800 flowers in his garden. He picked some flowers and now 349 are left in the garden. Of the flowers Dad picked, 43 are pink and the rest are white. How many white flowers did dad pick from his garden?*

Then we look again at the problem's context and agree it is not something our students will be invested in, so we decide to rewrite the problem to be about our school's upcoming annual fundraiser walk, but keep the same numbers and problem type.

> *Our school is hosting the annual Fun Run! There are 800 people there to cheer us on. At the end 349 people leave, but many are still on the turf to congratulate everyone; 43 of those people are parents and the rest are grandparents. How many grandparents are on the turf at the end of the Fun Run?*

Mark pulls up a photo from last year's Fun Run and puts it into our plans so we can help students visualize the problem.

Next we talk about how our students might solve this problem. Mark describes his forecast (how he thinks students will solve the problem based on his knowledge of the students, numbers, and problem type). "With the two steps, I think my students are going to subtract 349 from 800 first. They might decompose the 349 because they're really into using that strategy right now. So I think they will write 300, 40, 9. Then they will subtract each part from the 800. So, 800 − 300 = 500, 500 − 40 = 460, and 460 − 9 = 451."

"Yeah, some of my students will do that too." I respond. "I think decomposing is a strategy they used a lot in second grade. I also think a good amount of students will not subtract, but instead add up from 349 to 800."

"You're right. These numbers would make that strategy pretty simple actually," Mark notices.

"I wonder who will see that 349 as almost 350. Then, add 50 to make it 400 and 400 more to get to 800. Then, add the 1 + 50 + 400 = 451" I add.

"Wait, can you write that down?" Mark slows me down and we refocus on the Forecasting Guide sitting in front of me. The Forecasting Guide is a tool we use to record all the ways our students might solve a problem (Figure P.1). It is also a guidebook for us to refer to when we get stuck anticipating how students might solve. Later, during Grapple Time we will record our observations of how students actually solve on the Forecasting Guide and use it to reflect. Often filling out the Forecasting Guide with a partner or a team leads to conversations that help everyone better understand the math.

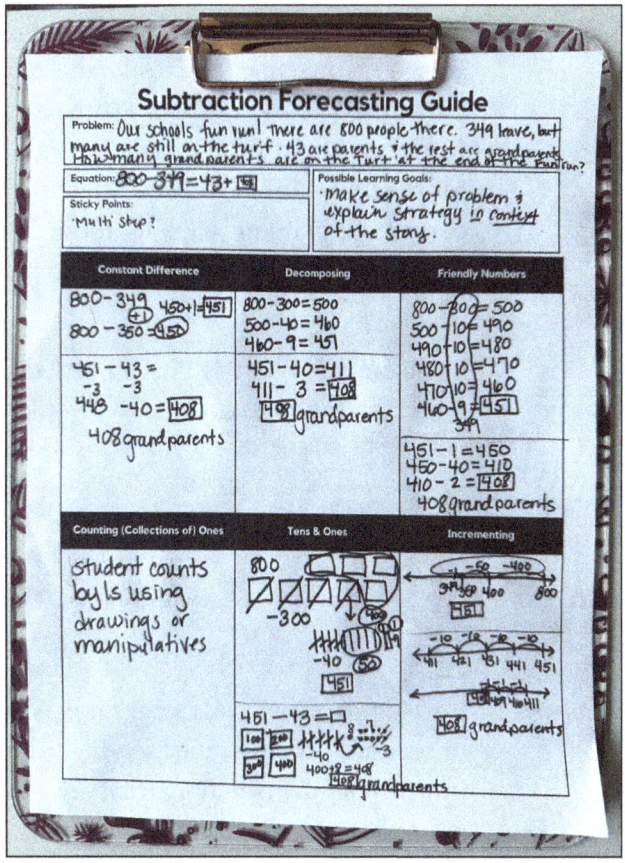

**FIGURE P.1** A Forecasting Guide helps teachers anticipate the strategies students will use to solve a problem.

Planning for Word Problem Workshop

After I show Mark the adding up strategy I described, we agree that some students may see this strategy as a preferred option to subtracting.

During this planning discussion, Mark and I also talk about any sticky spots or misconceptions we anticipate students might have. "I'm thinking the two steps might throw some kids off. I can think of a few kids who might shut down because they don't understand what's going on in the problem," I admit.

Mark agrees. "Yeah, let's plan to do a norms refresh conversation before we start. Let's remind them of what it looks like, sounds like and feels like to grapple. The last addition and subtraction problems we did were pretty easy and I didn't see as much grappling. We probably should have upped the rigor with those problems. Anyway, let's revisit what it means to grapple. Also, we'll really want to make sure we spend some time helping students retell and make sense of this problem in the Launch. I'll put it in the plans."

"That's making me think a goal for this problem is going to really be getting students to make sense of and understand the multiple steps. We might be able to hit on a few other goals in this Word Problem Workshop, but I think understanding the problem and how it relates to the strategies they choose is going to be first and foremost in this unit." I say. Mark agrees and we move on.

Finally, Mark jots down some additional numbers for this problem and works them out on the back of his Forecasting Guide so we can use them for the One More Problem reflection strategy (in Step 5: Reflect). This first part of our planning took us about fifteen minutes. We have four more days to plan so we keep going.

> **We can** plan for Word Problem Workshops that encourage students to think deeply and grapple as they problem solve—all in ways that are differentiated to meet students' unique needs and do not take a lot of time. Along the way, we'll build our own math understanding and confidence as well.

## Establish a Learning Goal for Word Problem Workshop

If we don't have a clear goal for a Word Problem Workshop, it runs the risk of becoming a drawn out solving time followed by a meandering discussion in which students may participate but don't learn much. On Episode 80 of my podcast, Math Chat (monamath.com/podcast/peg), I interviewed Margaret "Peg" Smith, the coauthor of *5 Practices for Orchestrating Productive Mathematics Discussions*. During our interview, Smith shared her take on

CCSS.MATH.CONTENT.5.NBT.B.6

(Find) whole-number quotients of whole numbers with up to four-digit dividends and two-digit divisors (using) strategies based on place value, the properties of operations, and/or the relationship between multiplication and division. (Illustrate) and (explain) the calculation by using equations, rectangular arrays, and/or area models.

**FIGURE P.2** Unpacking standards is a critical step in determining learning goals for Word Problem Workshop.

the importance of learning goals by saying they are the most important and perhaps the hardest element to plan. She emphasized how having a clear learning goal from the beginning influences the choices teachers make—like which student work to share and which questions to ask. Smith also weighed in on how we should write these learning goals, saying, "So as a teacher, separate what the student already has and what the piece is you need to help them work toward" (Iehl 2023). Pairing our understanding of the progression of mathematical ideas in our standards with our knowledge of our students, we can choose a learning goal that will ground Word Problem Workshop in meaningful learning for every student.

To create a learning goal for Word Problem Workshop, start by considering two key factors: 1) what your math standards require, and 2) what your students are showing they need next.

Here's a simple process for choosing a learning goal:

1. **Review** your curriculum, scope and sequence, and standards. Focus on the most important standards or content for your students, often called the major work or priority standards for the grade.

2. **Unpack** the standards by circling the verbs (what students must do) and underlining the key nouns (what they need to understand) (Figure P.2).

3. **Write** the big ideas and skills in the standard in your own words (Figure P.3).

### Big Ideas

- **Find quotients**
- **Strategies:** place value, properties of operations, relationships between multiplication & division
- **Models:** arrays, area model, equations
- **Show strategy on paper**
- **Explain on paper & in discussions**

**FIGURE P.3** Jotting down the big ideas in your own words after unpacking a standard will help you focus on what students need to know and be able to do in order to master that particular standard.

*Planning for Word Problem Workshop*

4. **Reflect** on students' needs, strengths, and experiences that they will bring to the work ahead.

5. **Select** a clear and focused learning goal.

Remember, each student's path to mastery is unique. Write down or discuss with a colleague what you know about your students' understandings of the unpacked standard and the big ideas you've identified. With this insight, you'll be ready to choose a learning goal that aligns with the standard, fits your students' needs, and pushes their learning forward.

### A Good Learning Goal
- Emphasizes what students need to learn
- Is aligned to grade-level standards
- Is relevant to students' current understanding

## In Action: Creating a Learning Goal

Let's take a look at what it might look like to plan a learning goal for a fifth-grade class that is currently working on decimal computation.

**Standard:**

5.NBT.B.7: Add, subtract, multiply, and divide decimals to hundredths, using concrete models or drawings and strategies based on place value, properties of operations, and/or the relationship between addition and subtraction; relate the strategy to a written method and explain the reasoning used.

**Standard Unpacked into Big Ideas:**
- All four operations with decimals to the hundredths
- Both concrete place value models (and manipulatives that might include money, base-ten blocks, place value disks) and visual models (place value chart, drawings of manipulatives)
- Strategies should draw on students' understandings of the properties of operations

- Represent their strategy on paper
- Explain reasoning on paper and in discussions

**Most of My Students:**
- Have experience with all four operations with whole numbers
- Have strong place value understanding with whole numbers
- Have experience with and excitement around money as an accessible and familiar way to think about decimals
- Are inexperienced with other decimal models and manipulatives (will need to introduce these)

**Today's Learning Goal:** Add decimals to hundredths place using strategies that draw on students' experiences with whole number addition.

## Choose a Word Problem for Word Problem Workshop

When you flip through your curriculum, you'll likely come across plenty of word problems. Pay attention to the word problems that students find "too hard" or skip altogether. These word problems are usually at the end of the problem set in the lesson. When you come across a problem you'd like to use, try revising it, just like Mark and I did in the opening story. If you don't find useful problems in your curriculum, you'll need to write your own. Whether you revise or write new problems you'll want to make sure to encourage productive struggle by avoiding prescribing a specific strategy or solution pathway. We want our word problems to entice students to dive in and experience the joy of "figuring it out" on their own and in collaboration with peers.

When planning a word problem:

- Remove any instructions that suggest strategies or models. Instead, encourage students to choose their own approach.
- Make sure the problem type you choose is aligned with your learning goal.
- Adjust the numbers responsively to meet your students' needs and grade-level learning goals.
- Make the context relatable to students or an opportunity to learn something new about others and the world.

## In Action: Revising a Word Problem from the Curriculum

Let's take a look at how a teacher revised a word problem from their curriculum for her class of second-grade students. The curriculum suggested the following word problem:

There are 27 candy bars and 18 students. Give one candy bar to each of the 18 students by crossing out candy bars in the picture above. How many are left over to share with the teachers?

While the teacher decided to keep the problem type (Separate Result Unknown), the numbers, and the context of the problem the same, she revised the problem to:

*There are 18 students in our class. We have a bag of 27 candy bars. If every student gets one candy bar how many will be left over to share with the teachers?*

Although both the original and the revised word problem ask students to solve 27 – 18 = ?, the curriculum word problem provides a pre-created model and dictates the strategy students should use. Even if you were to cross off that part of the directions or ask students to disregard the strategy suggestion, this task is not designed to generate rich problem solving and discussion. Because so much of the work has been done or heavily suggested to students in the curriculum's version of the problem, the solving experience is more likely to be focused on answers, not students' thinking.

The revised word problem, on the other hand, removes the pre-created model and directions, making it more open-ended. This version makes space for students to make sense of the problem and choose models and strategies for problem solving.

### Checklist for Revising a Word Problem

Find a curriculum task that you want to use. Then, use this checklist to revise it for Word Problem Workshop.

- Remove any pre-created models so that students can create their own, if desired
- Remove prompts or directions to use a certain strategy (i.e., "count on" or "cross out")
- Add an open answer space (Instead of _____ candy bars, try this: Answer: _____)
- Add an equation space for students to write in equations that match the problem and the way they solved it
- Revise the problem to include a context relevant to your students
- Change the problem type as needed

## Problem Types

There are many different types of problems. You might be thinking, yes of course—there are addition, subtraction, multiplication, and division problems. And if you're thinking that, you're right. Well, partially right.

In *Children's Mathematics: Cognitively Guided Instruction*, the authors share their research and classroom practice around fourteen different problem types and how students typically approach these problems (Carpenter et al. 2015). Within this Cognitively Guided Instruction framework, there are five categories of problem types: joining, separating, comparing, part-part-whole, and multiplication and division. Within each category, there are different problem types according to the location of the unknown quantity. For example, within the joining category, there are three problem types: Join Result Unknown (a + b = ?), Join Change Unknown (a + ? = c) and Join Start Unknown (? + b = c).

Understanding the different problem types and the strategies children frequently use to solve them allows teachers to choose problems that both support and challenge students' thinking (Carpenter et al. 2015). Take time to read through each problem type in Figures P.4 and P.5. Consider the location of the unknown in each problem type and how that might affect your students' strategies for solving.

### Addition and Subtraction Problem Types

Adapted from *Children's Mathematics: Cognitively Guided Instruction* (Carpenter et al. 2015)

**Join Problems:** Involve an action combining two or more quantities.

| Result Unknown | Change Unknown | Start Unknown |
|---|---|---|
| Ida has 4 dollars. Her mom gives her 18 more dollars. How many dollars does she have now? $4 + 18 = ?$ | Ida has 4 dollars. How much more money does she need to buy a stuffed animal that costs 22 dollars? $4 + ? = 22$ | Ida had a piggy bank with some money inside. Then she got 18 dollars for her birthday and put it in her piggy bank. Now she has 22 dollars. How much was in her bank before her birthday? $? + 18 = 22$ |

**Separate Problems:** Involve an action that decreases a quantity.

| Result Unknown | Change Unknown | Start Unknown |
|---|---|---|
| Mike had 15 cookies. He ate 8 of them on Monday. How many cookies does he have left? $15 - 8 = ?$ | Mike had 15 cookies. He ate some. He has 7 cookies left. How many did he eat? $15 - ? = 7$ | Mike has a plate of cookies. He ate 8 cookies. He has 7 left. How many cookies were on the plate to start? $? - 8 = 7$ |

**Part-Part-Whole Problems:** Involve relating parts to a whole. Unlike Join and Separate Problems there is no action in these problems.

| Whole Unknown | Part Unknown |
|---|---|
| There are 14 people on the Tigers team and 18 people on the Lions team. How many people are on both teams? $14 + 18 = ?$ | There are 32 people playing flag football; 14 people are on the Tigers team and the rest of the people are on the Lions team. How many are on the Lions team? $32 = 14 + ?$ |

**Compare Problems:** Involve comparing two quantities. Like Part-Part-Whole problems, Compare problems involve relationships rather than actions.

| Difference Unknown *Comparing two quantities, looking for the difference* | Compare Quantity Unknown *Comparing two quantities, but one quantity is unknown* | Referent Unknown *Comparing two quantities, but one quantity is compared to the difference* |
|---|---|---|
| Molly has 19 books. Mary has 14 books. How many more books does Molly have than Mary? $19 - 14 = ?$ or $14 + ? = 19$ | Molly has 19 books. Mary has 14 more books than Molly. How many books does Mary have? $19 + 14 = ?$ | Molly has 19 books. She has 7 more books than Mary. How many books does Mary have? $19 - 7 = ?$ or $? + 7 = 19$ |

**FIGURE P.4** Addition and subtraction problem types.

## Multiplication and Division Problem Types

Adapted from *Children's Mathematics: Cognitively Guided Instruction* (Carpenter et al. 2015)

| **Multiplication** Number of groups and amount per group is known, total is unknown | **Partitive Division** Number of groups and total is known, amount per group is unknown | **Measurement Division** The amount per group and total is known, number of groups is unknown |
|---|---|---|
| There are 9 groups of kids on the field trip. There are 7 kids in each group. How many kids are on the field trip? $9 \times 7 = ?$ | There are 63 kids on the field trip. The teacher splits them into 9 groups. How many kids are in each group? $63 \div 9 = ?$ | There are 63 kids on the field trip. The teacher puts 7 kids into each group. How many groups will there be? $63 \div 7 = ?$ |

**Other problem situations to note for Multiplication and Division:**

- **Multiplicative comparison problems:** The waterslide is 3 times as tall as the diving board. The diving board is 6 feet tall. How tall is the water slide?
- **Area problems:** The concert in the gym needs 5 rows of chairs. Each row needs 12 chairs. How many chairs are needed for the concert?
- **Measurement conversions:** How many inches are in 4 feet?
- **Unit rate:** A 3 pack of toy cars costs $7. What is the cost of one toy car?
- **Volume:** A fish tank is 12 inches long, 8 inches wide, and 10 inches tall. What is the total volume of the tank?

**FIGURE P.5** Multiplication and division problem types.

According to the Cognitively Guided Instruction research (and probably your own experiences as a teacher!), some problem types are more difficult to solve than others. For example, a Join Result Unknown problem is often one of the easier problem types for children to access because of the clear and familiar action in its structure. Because of the range in difficulty level between problem types, it is important to offer students experience with all types of problems. For example, you might revise a Join Result Unknown problem into a Join Change Unknown problem to give students experience solving a different kind of joining problem where the unknown is in a different location and the action can be more difficult for students to model. For example, let's take a look at this Join Result Unknown problem:

> *Rupert has 8 crackers at snack time. Then his mom gives him 4 more. How many crackers does Rupert have now?*

We could revise this problem to a Join Change Unknown problem:

> *Rupert has 8 crackers at snack time. Then his mom gives him some more crackers. Now he has 12 crackers. How many crackers did Rupert's mom give him?*

If the learning goal is focused on addition and Join Result Unknown is the only problem type students have solved, it is time to change up the problem type. Over the course of a few weeks, within a unit on addition and subtraction, you can offer students a variety of problem types to help them deepen their understanding. Figure P.6 illustrates three weeks of Word Problem Workshop plans in a first-grade class. The teacher chose Join, Separate, and Part-Part-Whole problem types to support her students in the learning goal of using place value to effectively solve addition and subtraction problems. Although the learning goal remains the same over the course of three weeks in this first-grade class, the problem types change to challenge students to apply their understanding in different problem situations.

| Standard | Big Ideas |
|---|---|
| **1.NBT.C.4**<br>Add within 100, including adding a two-digit number and a one-digit number, and adding a two-digit number and a multiple of 10, using concrete models or drawings and strategies based on place value, properties of operations, and/or the relationship between addition and subtraction; relate the strategy to a written method and explain the reasoning used. Understand that in adding two-digit numbers, one adds tens and tens, ones and ones; and sometimes it is necessary to compose a ten. | **Big Ideas from 1.NBT.C.4**<br>Add within 100<br>• Add a two-digit number and one-digit number<br>• Add a two-digit number and a multiple of 10 (for example: $34 + 20 = ?$)<br>• Models: Concrete and visual<br>• Strategies that draw on: Place value, properties of operations, relationship between addition/subtraction<br>• Show strategy on paper<br>• Explain reasoning |
| **1.NBT.C.6**<br>Subtract multiples of 10 in the range 10–90 from multiples of 10 in the range 10–90 (positive or zero differences), using concrete models or drawings and strategies based on place value, properties of operations, and/or the relationship between addition and subtraction; relate the strategy to a written method and explain the reasoning used. | **Big Ideas from NBT.C.6**<br>• Subtract multiples of 10 between 10 and 90 (for example $60 - 40 = ?$)<br>• Models: Concrete and visual<br>• Strategies that draw on: Place value, properties of operations, relationship between addition/subtraction<br>• Show strategy on paper<br>• Explain reasoning |
| **Learning Goal:** Use multiple strategies to describe the relationship between addition and subtraction |||

| WEEK 1 | Problem Type | Equation | Word Problem |
|---|---|---|---|
| **Monday** | Join Result Unknown | | |

**FIGURE P.6** This addition and subtraction unit plan shows how the teacher aligned the standards, big ideas, and problem types. The teacher will add numbers and contexts next. *(Continued)*

| | | | |
|---|---|---|---|
| Tuesday | Join Result Unknown | | |
| Wednesday | Part-Part-Whole, Whole Unknown | | |
| Thursday | Part-Part-Whole, Whole Unknown | | |
| **WEEK 2** | **Problem Type** | **Equation** | **Word Problem** |
| Monday | Separate Change Unknown | | |
| Tuesday | Separate Change Unknown | | |
| Wednesday | Part-Part-Whole, Part Unknown | | |
| Thursday | Part-Part-Whole, Part Unknown | | |
| **WEEK 3** | **Problem Type** | **Equation** | **Word Problem** |
| Monday | Join Change Unknown | | |
| Tuesday | Join Change Unknown | | |
| Wednesday | Join Start Unknown | | |
| Thursday | Join Start Unknown | | |

**FIGURE P.6** *(Continued)*

### In Action: Planning for Problem Types

When planning for several weeks of Word Problem Workshop it's helpful to chart out the problems over the course of the weeks so you can make sure you're offering students a variety of different problem types.

Now let's take a look at another example of how a third-grade teacher has planned for a variety of problem types across a multiplication and division unit (Figure P.7).

| Standard | Big Ideas |
|---|---|
| **3.OA.A.3** Use multiplication and division within 100 to solve word problems in situations involving equal groups, arrays, and measurement quantities, e.g., by using drawings and equations with a symbol for the unknown number to represent the problem. | Multiply and divide within 100<br>• Problem contexts: Equal groups, arrays, measurement quantities<br>• Models: Visual and equations<br>• Write equations to show the unknown |

**Learning Goal:** Write an equation that matches the problem and your strategy for solving. Explain why your equation matches the problem and/or your strategy.

| WEEK 1 | Problem Type | Equation | Word Problem |
|---|---|---|---|
| **Monday** | Multiplication | | |
| **Tuesday** | Multiplication | | |
| **Wednesday** | Measurement Division | | |
| **Thursday** | Measurement Division | | |
| **WEEK 2** | **Problem Type** | **Equation** | **Word Problem** |
| **Monday** | Partitive Division | | |
| **Tuesday** | Partitive Division | | |
| **Wednesday** | Multiplication (larger numbers) | | |
| **Thursday** | Multiplication (larger numbers) | | |
| **WEEK 3** | **Problem Type** | **Equation** | **Word Problem** |
| **Monday** | Partitive Division | | |
| **Tuesday** | Partitive Division | | |
| **Wednesday** | Measurement Division | | |
| **Thursday** | Measurement Division | | |

**FIGURE P.7** This multiplication and division unit plan shows how the teacher aligned the standards, big ideas and problem types. The teacher will add numbers and contexts next.

Here are some additional tips for choosing word problems for Word Problem Workshop:

- Bundle two problems of the same problem type together so students can apply their learning from the first day to the second day's problem.
- Switch problem types after two days to keep students nimble with making sense of problems. When we do the same problem type over and over some students fall into the habit of applying a strategy without making sense of the problem first.
- Group like problem type categories together to practice a learning goal over several weeks (for example, joining, separating and part-part-whole problems for a unit on addition and subtraction).

## Intentional Number Choice

Once you've decided on your problem types it's time to select numbers for your problems with intention and thoughtfulness. The numbers you select should encourage progress toward the learning goal; choose numbers that all of your students can access, but are not too challenging.

The size of the numbers you choose can be guided by your grade-level standards. For example, in the Common Core Standards, for addition and subtraction word problems, first-grade students work within 20, second-grade students within 100, and third-grade students within 1,000. As part of unpacking your standards, take note of the size of numbers that are appropriate for your grade-level goals.

After choosing the relative size of the number you want to offer students in your word problems, you'll want to think intentionally about the exact numbers you choose. Different numbers will encourage the use of different strategies and can help your students uncover the big ideas of mathematics. For example, if most of your students solved the problem $38 + 11 = ?$ with strategies that show understanding of place value (such as $30 + 10 = 40$, $8 + 1 = 9$, $40 + 9 = 49$) along with clear models and explanations, then you may want to try numbers that encourage thinking about regrouping. Perhaps the number problem could be $49 + 16 = ?$ These numbers nudge students to consider what to do when the sum of the ones is greater than ten ($9 + 6 = 15$, in this example). By thoughtfully choosing the numbers in your word problems you can encourage students to work toward the learning goal. In Figure P.8 I offer other ways intentional number choice might encourage students to try out new strategies and develop deeper mathematical understanding.

| A Few Examples of How Intentional Number Choice Can Encourage Students to Try New Strategies and Build Understanding ||
|---|---|
| **Intentional Number Choice** | **Can Encourage Students to...** |
| When writing addition problems, try offering numbers that include zeros such as:<br><br>409 + 50<br>30 + 12 | Decompose by place value<br><br>Make jumps of 10 or 100 from a given number |
| When writing addition problems, try offering problems where one number is very close to a ten or hundred. | Use compensation when adding—take some quantity from one number and give it to another to make the problem easier to work with.<br><br>**59 + 63 =**<br>+1   −1<br>60 + 62 = 122 |
| When writing subtraction problems, try offering problems where the minuend (number being subtracted from) ends in zeros. | Use constant difference when subtracting—adding or subtracting the same amount to both numbers in a subtraction problem in order to create an equivalent, but easier problem to solve.<br><br>**500 − 189**<br>  −1    −1<br>499 − 188 = 311 |
| When writing division problems, try offering numbers that result in remainders. | Reason about what should be done with the remainder. Depending on the context of the word problem, students might make a remainder a fraction, decimal, round up, or think of the remainder as "leftovers." |
| When writing any type of problem, consider sometimes using numbers that are smaller or larger than those with which students typically work. | With smaller numbers: Reason and make sense of the context of a harder problem type, without worrying too much about the computation part.<br><br>With larger numbers: Take on a challenge that some students might be ready for. |
| When writing any type of word problem, consider offering problems that progress in complexity over time. | Build skills and confidence with similar problems over time.<br><br>By starting with simpler numbers and progressing to more difficult ones later in the week or unit, you will create an onramp for all students to access the problem and build skills across multiple Word Problem Workshops. |
| When writing any type of word problem, consider offering number choices. | Take leadership over their learning by choosing numbers that challenge them appropriately. You can provide sets of number options from which students can choose.<br><br>A first-grade problem might look like this:<br><br>*Millie the dog has a _____ ounce bowl full of water. She drinks some water after being outside. Now Millie's bowl has _____ ounces of water in it. How much water did Millie drink?*<br><br>(32, 19) (16, 5) |

**FIGURE P.8** Some ways to think intentionally about number choice in word problems.

## The Context of the Problem

Understanding the context is one part of word problems that can hold our students back from solving. We know our students will encounter tricky contexts on standardized assessments, so it is important we make sure the context is relevant to their lives, but also realistically prepares them for the tasks they will encounter in school. In Word Problem Workshop we strive for a balance between helping students see the world of interesting problems that exist in their lives, while also being prepared for the realities of the world of "school math."

A relatable problem context engages students by reflecting their own experiences or offering a glimpse into someone else's world. As Dr. Rudine Sims Bishop explains in "Mirrors, Windows, and Sliding Glass Doors," students need texts that act as mirrors, reflecting their identities and communities, as well as texts that are windows, providing insight into other people's lived experiences (1990). While Bishop's work focused on these ideas within children's literature, the same is true in math class and of word problems as a kind of text with which students engage. Using diverse contexts in math problems fosters understanding, empathy, and the development of problem-solving skills.

Sometimes the context of word problems can help students understand difficult math content. Measurement contexts, for example, can be challenging for students to understand—whether it is length, time, capacity, area, or volume. Relatable contexts can help students build background knowledge about how measurement is used beyond the classroom. For example, you might draw on students' favorite play activities and informal understandings about measurement to write a problem such as:

> *Julian was testing how far his toy cars could go down the ramp. He placed a mark where each car finished. The red car went 68 inches. The blue car went 93 inches. How many more inches did the blue car travel than the red car?*

Writing problem contexts that incorporate less familiar math concepts (such as inches as a unit of measurement) gives students exposure to these ideas, while also making the math come to life.

## Planning by Doing the Math

How do you feel when you're asked to "do the math" during a professional development session? If you've ever felt dread, insecurity, or even shame in those moments, you're not alone. I've been there too. These feelings are common among teachers. Many elementary teachers like us enter the field ready to teach almost anything except math, despite having college courses and certifications under our belts. Why? Because so many of us carry the belief, "I'm just not a math person."

For many of us as students, math was taught as a series of rigid steps and rules to memorize, not as a subject full of discovery and sense-making. Asking *why* something works was discouraged in favor of simply following the procedures to get the right answer. Now, as teachers, we're faced with the challenge of teaching math in a way that feels different from how we learned it—and that can feel unsettling. Our discomfort may lead us to rely on scripts and slides, further perpetuating the cycle we experienced—some students thriving while others quietly (or not-so-quietly) disengage, thinking "Math just isn't for me." Without time or support to reflect on our own math past, our pedagogy may remain rooted in survival and avoidance rather than empowerment and connection.

We can't plan meaningful lessons until we've done the math ourselves. To help students make sense of problems and support them in grappling and discussing, we must first walk the problem-solving pathway. By doing so, we prepare ourselves to support students' thinking and, in some cases, begin healing our own relationship with math.

## *Forecasting Students' Strategies*

In college, I learned that anticipatory sets are activities at the beginning of a lesson to engage students and connect their prior knowledge to the current lesson. However, I didn't realize that anticipating could also be a powerful tool for lesson planning until I read *5 Practices for Orchestrating Productive Math Discussions* (Smith and Stein 2018). The authors describe anticipation as a key practice in which teachers consider how students might approach a problem. Anticipating helps us plan by encouraging teachers to do the math themselves, preparing for students' possible strategies, misconceptions, and questions we might ask students.

My experience has shown me that it's nearly impossible to predict *every* way a student might solve a problem. After years of anticipating strategies and responses, I still walk into classrooms and find students using unexpected strategies or models. (And honestly, these surprises can be part of the joy of teaching!) That's why I now take the pressure off myself and other teachers by reframing this step of planning as forecasting.

Like forecasting the weather, forecasting students' strategies is our best effort to predict what might happen, while knowing the wind could change direction or the skies might surprise us with unexpected sunshine. We can't anticipate exactly what students will do, think, or try when problem solving. However, when we forecast how students *might* solve we can stay nimble and open to shifting our approach as we facilitate Word Problem Workshop. The forecast helps us plan for how we will support and guide students while staying flexible to their ideas and approaches.

## Models and Strategies

Students can model their math thinking in many ways, even while using the same strategy. If a student is solving the problem 48 + 23 with the strategy of decomposing by place values (Figure P.9), they may use a physical, visual, or symbolic model to show their strategy. A physical model could include using counters, snap cubes, or ten frames to break apart and add 48 and 23 by place value. A student could also use a visual model by drawing base-ten blocks or a number line. Finally, a student could use a symbolic model, using only equations to represent their strategy.

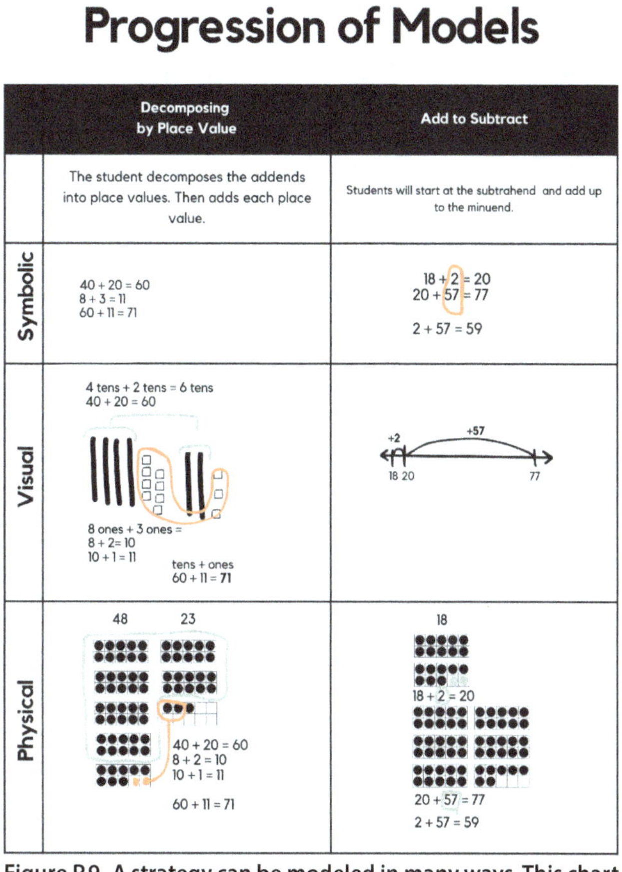

It is important to note that, over time, students will progress through models based on a number of factors (Figure P.10). New material, unfamiliar problem types, or larger numbers are a few reasons students might use a physical or visual model. When I was teaching third grade many of my students were using symbolic models for addition and subtraction. However, when multiplication and division was introduced, students started using physical and visual models to solve those problems. After several weeks of comparing different models and discussing the efficiency of each, students started to understand the big ideas and naturally experimented with more efficient, symbolic models.

**Figure P.9** A strategy can be modeled in many ways. This chart shows an example of a physical, visual, and symbolic model for two different strategies.

## Considering Math Progressions and Learning Trajectories

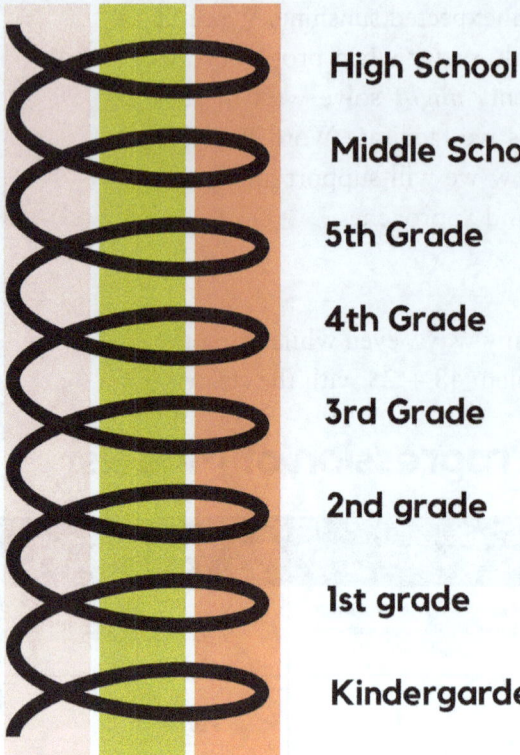

**FIGURE P.10** Depending on the math concept, context, and numbers in a problem, students may use a physical, visual, or symbolic model to represent their strategy.

It can be a challenging task (even for adults!) to sit down with a problem and solve it in multiple ways. After all our years of schooling and practice, we each have our own preferred strategies. Sometimes we may feel stumped after jotting down one or two strategies or may be inclined to stick to the strategies presented in our curriculum. Instead, we can challenge ourselves to push beyond these limits and consider the variety of strategies students may use. While our curriculum may provide a clear progression of skills and strategies, the reality is that each child is on their own learning trajectory. True learning trajectories are often nonlinear, and vary depending on each individual's experiences, challenges, and strengths. An individual's learning trajectory might be less predictable than a progression, as it reflects a student's unique growth in their understanding. As illustrated in Figure P.11, while a progression (often found in our curriculum and standards) helps us order math concepts from more simple to more complex according

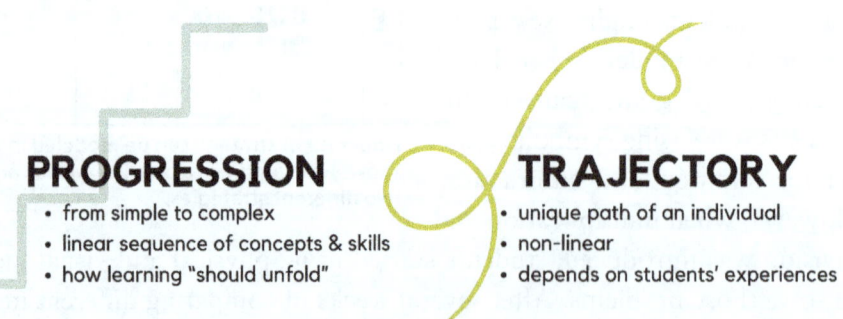

Figure P.11 Understanding progressions of mathematical concepts and skills helps educators support students on their learning trajectories.

to our grade level, students' individual trajectories are often messier! In Word Problem Workshop we provide students an opportunity to embrace their own learning journey, making progress on their trajectory guided by learning goals aligned to the progression. The better we understand the progression of mathematical ideas, the more equipped we are to support each student on their individual trajectory.

Many educators have spent time researching the progressions of mathematics and translating this research into accessible professional learning for teachers. Graham Fletcher's progression videos show how students develop mathematical thinking through the school years with models and strategies (gfletchy.com/progression-videos/). Pam Harris's blog post discusses how reasoning builds from early childhood through high school (www.mathisfigureoutable.com/blog/development).

## *Forecasting Guide*

The goal is to make forecasting simple and effective so that we can do this work each week as we plan for Word Problem Workshop. The Forecasting Guide templates are designed to reflect the math learning progression. Notice in Figure P.12 six strategies students might use to solve. Of course, these are not the only strategies your students might use, but they are a good starting point to get you familiar with the progression of strategies and models. The goal is to create an easy to use, one-page forecast of potential strategies and models students might use to solve the problem. Once you've sketched out the possible ways students will solve, you'll look for connections between strategies, questions to ask, and potential sticky spots for students.

Figure P.12 The Forecasting Guide for addition problems. Forecasting Guides for addition, subtraction, multiplication, and division are all available in the online resources.

*Planning for Word Problem Workshop* **175**

## Strategies for Subtraction

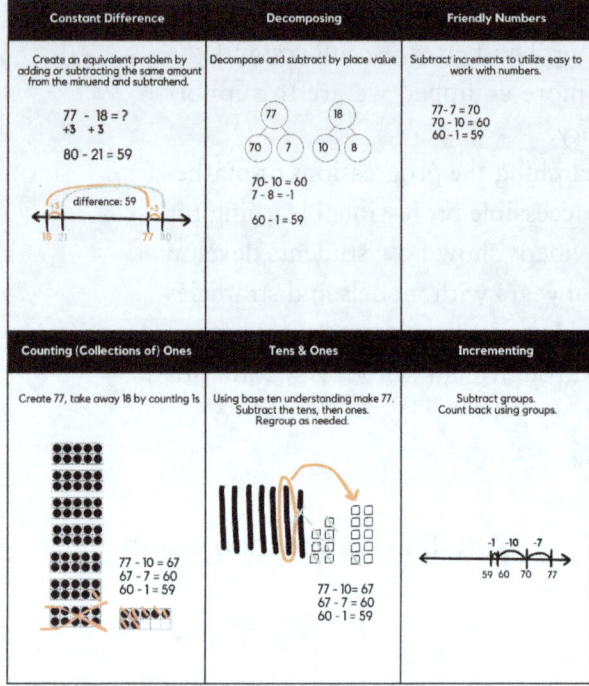

**FIGURE P.13** It is helpful to complete a Forecasting Guide when planning to consider how students might solve the problem. You'll find completed Forecasting Guides in the online resources to aid you in your planning.

## Forecasting Connections, Questions, and Sticky Spots

As you solve the problem and consider the progression of strategies and models, notice connections between strategies, questions you might ask students, and sticky spots students might run into. As you take a moment to recognize connections between different strategies and models, you might, for example, notice that the visual model (the open number line, in this case) takes the same "hops" that are present within the symbolic equations as well (Figure P.13). Or maybe you see the connection that the strategy of subtracting to get to a multiple of ten can be represented with physical, visual, and symbolic models. Make note of these connections because they will help you decide whose work to select to share. When the connection aligns with the learning goal, you'll be able to select students to bring the connection to life on the chart paper and in the Discussion. There may be many options here. You aren't deciding anything now. You'll use this completed Forecasting Guide during Grapple Time to make notes of what you observe and then ultimately select student work to share based on what students are doing during Grapple Time.

As you work through the Forecasting Guide, you can also think about the questions you might ask students during Grapple Time or the Discussion. Our questions can encourage students' thinking and nudge them toward more efficient or effective strategies and models. If my student was solving by counting all by ones, I might ask, "Is there a more efficient way to count those blocks?" This question might encourage the student to count up or even look for ways to make a ten. Figure P.14 shows how the student who was previously using manipulatives to count all by ones shifted to a made a ten strategy. I might ask the student about this shift by saying, "What happened here when you moved these three yellow counters onto the ten frame?"

176  Word Problem Workshop

Sticky spots include potential confusions students might have, mistakes they might make, and common misconceptions that might arise as they solve. Make a note of these on your Forecasting Guide as you plan. Then, be on the lookout for them during Grapple Time. If students run into a sticky spot, you might stop the class during Grapple Time and say, "Hey everyone, look up here real quick. [Pointing to the problem on the board] I notice that some folks are running into the same confusion. Let's look back at the problem. I'm going to read it and I want you to think about which quantities represent the number of groups, the size of those groups, and the total." By helping students refocus on understanding the context of the problem, the teacher intervenes and hopefully sets most students back onto a productive solving pathway.

**FIGURE P.14** Forecasting questions can guide us as we confer with students.

## *Observations and Data*

Completed Forecasting Guides become the guidebook for Word Problem Workshop. The Forecasting Guide includes how students may solve potential sticky spots, questions to ask, and connections to keep in mind when conferencing with students as they work. And carrying that Forecasting Guide with you on a clipboard during Grapple Time can serve another purpose—data collection.

During Grapple Time, walk around and notice what strategies and models students are using. Jot their names or initials into the box that aligns with their strategy. When you reach the end of Grapple Time, look back over your notes. Look for trends, outliers, and commonalities. As you decide who to select for the Share, use your observational data to guide you. For example, for the problem in Figure P.13 you could choose one student to share who used friendly numbers and a visual model, like a number line, and another student who used an invented algorithm that also capitalized on friendly numbers.

A Forecasting Guide from one Word Problem Workshop (like in Figure P.15) can be used to plan your next Word Problem Workshop as well. Looking back at the formative data collected can inform the selection of future learning goals, problem types, and numbers in problems. This formative data also can help you notice trends in student thinking. Over time, you can notice how students' strategies and models have progressed.

### In Action: Forecasting Guides

Let's take a look at the completed Forecasting Guide in Figure P.15. The majority of students in this second-grade class are drawing base-ten blocks (a visual model) to create friendly numbers when adding. However, four students are attempting symbolic models of their strategy by using equations. Notice how Leelah decomposed the numbers to add. Alitza and Evan added up to friendly numbers. Alice is incrementing by tens to add up. There is a connection between what most students are doing (using base-ten blocks to make friendly numbers to add) and what Alice, Leelah, Alitza, and Evan are doing. When deciding who will share, we might choose one of the many students who used base-ten blocks in order to make connections between their strategy and Leelah's and Evan's strategies.

Additional note: when many students all use the same strategy, this is a good time to select someone who may not have been chosen recently to share their strategy.

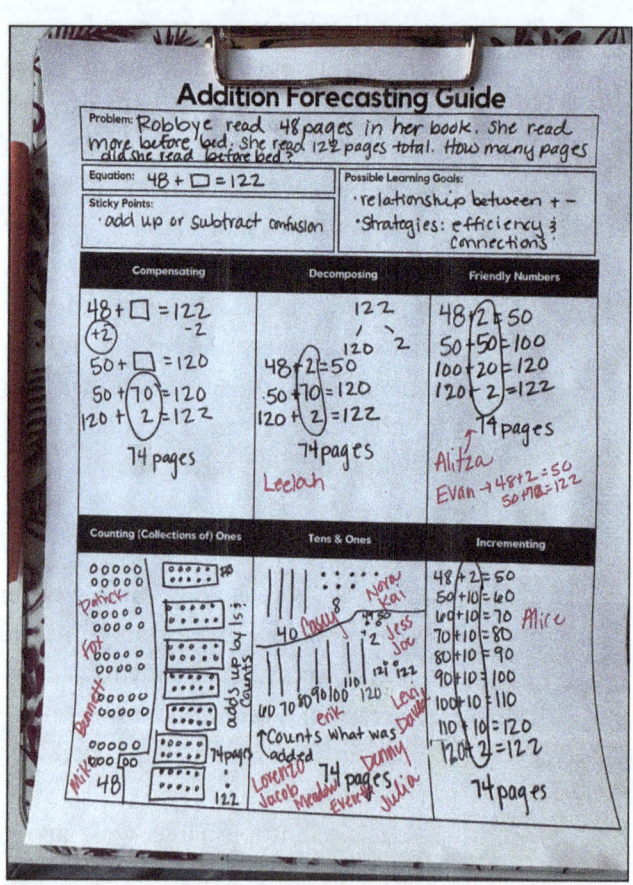

**FIGURE P.15** Forecasting Guides support teachers' work during Grapple Time and the Discussion. They help us think through the choices we will make and questions we will ask when facilitating students' thinking.

## *Making Forecasting a Habit*

In my experience, forecasting in partnerships or teams is most helpful. When forecasting with a grade-level team or math coach you'll be able to share ideas and help one another. You might be tempted to skip this part of planning. However, forecasting is essential to ensuring that Word Problem Workshop supports every learner in the development of deeper ideas. If our goal is to nudge and support each student to deeper understanding, then we must spend time considering the connections among ideas, strategies, and models. As you repeat this process over time, it will become more efficient and second nature for you.

## Plan in a Prep Period

Let's put all the pieces of this chapter together and discuss how you can fit an entire week of planning into one prep period. As a teacher myself, I completely understand that the hour you're given to plan each day (if you're lucky!) is actually about forty-three minutes once you walk students to and from music, stop to say hello to the parent in the hallway, and use the bathroom on your way back to close your door to plan math. However, if you remember the opening story of this chapter, my colleague Mark and I planned a week of Word Problem Workshop for our third-grade classes in one planning period. I promise you that it is possible.

**FIGURE P.16** Use this process to plan Word Problem Workshop during your prep period.

Choose one day a week to plan math for the next week. Then, follow the steps below (and see Figure P.16) to get your planning for Word Problem Workshop completed!

## *Step 1: Choose the Learning Goals*

Look through your unit plan, standards, and any goals for the week. Based on the curriculum and resources available at your school, you will choose a learning goal. Write the goal you will use for the week at the top of the Forecasting Guide.

*Planning for Word Problem Workshop* **179**

## Step 2: Choose the Problems

Find the word problems that will help you accomplish the goals. Decide on at least two problem types. Revise any problems you find in your curriculum. Write the problems at the top of your Forecasting Guide. Don't forget to write problems for your One More Problem (during the Reflection step of Word Problem Workshop). These One More Problems will use the same context as your problem for Word Problem Workshop, just different numbers.

## Step 3: Forecast

Solve the problems in as many ways as you can by completing the Forecasting Guide(s). As you do this, consider what your students will likely do, be confused by, or places they may get stuck.

## Step 4: Connections, Questions, and Sticky Spots

Notice connections between strategies and models and the learning goal. Consider how you might help students reach the goal by using and discussing the strategies and models. Make note of any questions you might ask students along the way. Anticipate any misconceptions, areas of confusion, or common mistakes that might come up with these problems.

## Step 5: Prepare Materials

Each student needs a copy of the problem. Print the problem on a strip of paper so students can cut and paste it into their notebooks. Or, give students a full sheet of paper with the problem typed at the top (Figure P.17). There are many creative options for managing materials. I've found what works best is finding an easy routine that makes sense for you.

Place the necessary manipulatives into table bins or individual bins for students to access easily. Write the problem at the top of the chart paper. Or to save time, print the problem and tape it to the top of the chart.

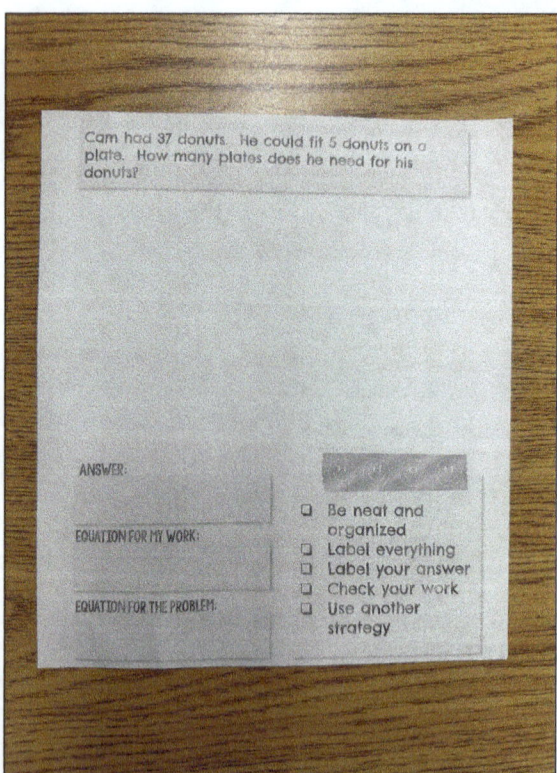

**FIGURE P.17** One way to present problems for Word Problem Workshop.

# Common Questions from Teachers

## What if I Have a Curriculum That I'm Required to Use?

Word Problem Workshop works with any curriculum because it is an instructional strategy, not a curriculum. This approach is designed to help you make the most of your talents, your students' abilities, and the curriculum resources available to you. Most curricula include problematic word problems that cause students to freeze, get bored, or give up. By using Word Problem Workshop, in just twenty minutes each day, students can work through word problems with confidence.

In my classroom, I've used Word Problem Workshop with various curricula, including traditional, problem-based, and scripted ones. All presented word problems in ways that led students to shut down. Instead of giving up, we tackled the toughest problems using Word Problem Workshop. My students gained confidence, improved their problem-solving skills, and became more willing to engage with difficult problems. When we returned to the curriculum workbook, they solved the problems by grappling, showing their thinking, and explaining their reasoning. Word Problem Workshop proved to be the best approach for teaching math, regardless of the curriculum.

## Where Do I Get the Problems?

There is no shortage of word problems out there. You'll certainly find a plethora of word problems in your curriculum and you can also adapt and write your own word problems that honor students' interests and shared experiences at school and beyond. Start with the curriculum and the resources you are provided by your school. Even if your curriculum isn't working as intended or you heavily modify or supplement it with additional resources, it still likely contains some thoughtfully written word problems that can be used (or revised) for Word Problem Workshop.

You can use the checklist on page 163 to help you evaluate the word problems in your curriculum for quality and revise them to be perfect for Word Problem Workshop. Don't be afraid to give the problems in your curriculum a glow-up by revising them!

Additionally, armed with the knowledge of the problem types we learned about earlier in this chapter, you can write word problems yourself. Teacher-created problems allow you to consider the numbers, contexts, and problem types that will help your students achieve the learning goals.

However, as a teacher myself I know how limited time is and especially for writing math problems. That's why I have an entire year of problems available for teachers to try out. You can find a month of problems in the online resources for this book.

### Can I Use Just One Part of Word Problem Workshop?

Yes, of course. All of the parts of Word Problem Workshop are research-informed instructional practices. Incorporating any of the steps into your math lessons will enhance students' experiences in math class. Start with one part of Word Problem Workshop and then add on another. Refer to the Getting Started Guide in the online resources for more tips. But don't stop at just one step, because the five steps of Word Problem Workshop work together to transform the way students problem solve and significantly increase their mathematical proficiency. In hundreds of classrooms across the country, teachers have used this approach to empower students to see word problems not as a chore, but as an exciting opportunity for real-world problem solving.

### I Like Math and Am Confident in My Skills, Do I Really Need to Do the Forecasting Guide?

I'm so grateful for elementary teachers, like you, who love math and have confidence in their abilities. You are a great asset to your school, colleagues, and students. You have the opportunity to take this instructional approach and run with it without the barrier of overcoming feelings of inadequacy. You'll be able to dive into this approach quickly!

That being said, forecasting helps everyone prepare for Word Problem Workshop—the teacher who has been doing this work for thirty years, the new teacher who is hesitant about teaching math, and everyone else in between. Forecasting isn't just about increasing your confidence in knowing the math, or understanding the strategies. It is about walking the solution pathways with your students in mind. Each year, heck, each day, our students are different and when we plan with them in mind our instruction is more impactful. So, I encourage you to team up with a colleague who perhaps doesn't share your same math confidence and forecast together. The planning will help both of you be prepared to support and challenge each of your students, and your enthusiasm will support your colleague in finding the joy in planning math.

# Be an Action Taker

## First Steps

- Be open to solving problems in many ways. As you plan, push yourself to solve in ways that might not be natural to you, but might be your students' preferred strategy.

- Find a problem in your curriculum that you can use to launch Word Problem Workshop. Will you use this problem as it is written or make some revisions?

- Solve the problem before you give it to students and consider how your students might approach the problem and the strategies they may use.

## Ready to Run

- Unpack a standard you are currently teaching and create a learning goal for Word Problem Workshop.

- Use a Forecasting Guide to plan, considering the questions you'll ask and connections between strategies.

- As you observe students during Grapple Time, use your Forecasting Guide to record the strategies students are using. Reflect on the trends you notice in your observations and in students' work. Use this information to select students for the Share and to plan for your next Word Problem Workshop.

# Conclusion: You're Ready to Inspire Problem Solvers in Your Classroom

Five educators stood in a loose circle outside of the first-grade classroom, their voices low as they shared anecdotes about siblings of their own students in this classroom. There was a hum of anticipation in the air as the teachers quietly discussed what to focus on and what to capture in their notes. The purpose of this day's visit to Ms. Jill's class was to observe evidence of students' thinking, but none of the teachers knew quite what to expect.

As we walked in, the faint sound of paper rustling and the scratches of pencils filled the air. Some students' eyes popped up from papers, their faces lighting up with sudden recognition—those must be the siblings. They flashed quick smiles and tiny waves, a brief interruption before they turned their focus back to the task at hand. The room was nearly silent, an almost peaceful hum, with the occasional whispers of two students talking about their strategies. Over at a desk near the windows, another student was conferring with Ms. Jill, her voice was gentle as she nudged the student to think through the problem.

As we walked through the desks, the first graders eagerly waved us over. One child pointed to their set of two-sided counters arranged into ten frames. Another student showed how he represented the snap cubes with a drawing on his paper. Two other students boasted about the equations they had created that matched their work and the problem. Every child's strategy was clearly represented in their manipulatives or drawings on their paper.

Ms. Jill walked around listening intently, getting curious about her students' thinking and offering nudges. She looked at us and smiled, making a passing comment about how hard it was to not just *show* them what to do, "but now I know it's *so* worth it," she gushed, her words trailing off as her eyes flicked back to the students grappling.

Later in the debrief of the learning walk it was Ms. Jill's colleagues' turn to gush about the student thinking they saw her facilitating.

"Every child was showing their thinking. I've never seen that in a first-grade class."

"Kids were getting stuck, but they weren't crying or even getting upset. That doesn't even happen in fifth grade! There's always a few with big feelings."

"Yeah, I had a conversation with a first grader about their strategies. That child said, 'We take a deep breath and remember we are smart and can do hard things. Then, we get back to work and try something else. It's okay when that happens.'"

"Evidence of student thinking was on their papers and manipulatives, but also on the chart Ms. Jill made with them."

"I saw charts all over the room from previous lessons. It's clear it's a routine."

"Did you hear how they talked about their strategies? My own six-year-old doesn't compare and contrast like they were doing in the turn and talk."

"I'm not sure if I heard the same kids you did, but I heard students talking about how efficient the second strategy was because she composed a ten and then counted on. They knew exactly what the student did and why she made those choices. I was impressed."

"They must have really been listening during the Share. I'm not sure my students listen that well. We've got work to do."

This is an example of how the movement spreads. It just takes one teacher to show that it is possible for students to lead the learning with the guidance of a passionate facilitator. It just takes one teacher to show that students are capable of more than they ever thought possible—to learn to solve complex problems while joyfully and productively engaging in struggle. It just takes one teacher to try something different and commit to coursing a different path for our students than we had in math class. Then, the next thing you know, we're all trusting kids, providing time for exploration, and showing our students that they are capable of being mathematicians. This school did it, why not yours? You're that one teacher.

## You Have the Tools to Inspire Curiosity and Confidence

When you started reading this book, I promised that Word Problem Workshop would help you create a classroom full of confident problem solvers—a place where students are motivated to tackle word problems, supported by their learning community and guided by you, their thoughtful facilitator. Now you have the tools to transform your classroom into a thriving math community where problem solving happens every day in math.

You are empowered to make your math classroom different from how it used to be or how it was when you were a student. You've embraced the opportunity to transform your teaching practice and your students' learning into opportunities to think deeply, explore new ideas, and discuss math reasoning. You understand that a student-centered approach inspires students to take ownership of their math learning. You're committed to honoring students' expertise and providing opportunities for students to explore problems with curiosity and confidence in their abilities. You've witnessed how mathematical discussions build students' math understanding and their ability to communicate effectively. You know that productive struggle is essential for deep learning. And you understand that connecting math to the world around us builds essential problem-solving skills they will carry beyond your class. In doing this work, you are preparing students to become the problem solvers our world needs.

Beyond shifting your approach, you've also gained the skills and strategies to implement a highly effective Word Problem Workshop that leaves students understanding more math and motivated to do hard things. Within each of the five steps of Word Problem Workshop, you have a simple set of strategies to follow. The five moves in the Launch will help students pack their backpack with everything they need to be ready to solve the problem. During Grapple Time, you have the tools to lay a solid foundation that will prepare students to persevere when they inevitably face challenges. You also have the moves to facilitate and support your students' thinking. During the Share, you have strategies to position everyone to learn from the students you selected to share their work. In the Discussion, you have the questions, prompts, and engagement moves to get every child meaningfully engaged in sharing their thinking and analyzing the perspectives of others. You can adapt the Discussion Framework as your facilitation develops.

You have the tools to help students reflect on their learning and apply it to new contexts and problems. During Reflect you can confidently provide students with feedback, knowing they can apply it to their learning in the next Word Problem Workshop.

Finally, you have the tools to thoughtfully put the pieces together to plan a purposeful and effective Word Problem Workshop. You can build your understanding of strategies and models through forecasting, considering questions, sticky spots, and connections your students may make on their problem-solving journey. With these strategies, you'll confidently guide students on their path to becoming empowered problem solvers.

Teaching word problems might have left you feeling overwhelmed and depleted in the past, with students struggling for a variety of reasons. But now, after reading this book, you don't have to feel that way anymore. You now know how to help students feel confident solving word problems.

If you started reading this book anything like past me—or the thousands of teachers like us—you felt like an imposter in math class. Not identifying as a "math person" made me feel unqualified to teach math.

Now, not only do you have the tools to use Word Problem Workshop in your classroom, you also have the confidence to continue learning and growing. One thing I've noticed from the teachers I've coached is that when they learn this approach, it propels them to learn even more. Many teachers are now experts at facilitating problem solving in ways that are better than me, their math coach! They have surpassed their mentor, and it won't be long before you do too.

Many people believe there is only one "right" way to learn math—the way they were taught. You may have heard, "If it worked for me, it will work for my kids." What these people might not realize is that many of us were failed by that way of learning math. The truth is, our traditional system and methods have never worked for most learners—and they still don't. Math doesn't have to stay the same. We have a better way.

You are now prepared to help your students develop as problem solvers and empower them to face the challenges of the world with confidence.

You'll guide them to get back up when they fail, to use the mathematical knowledge they do have to reason through problems they might not yet fully understand. You are now fulfilling the best role a teacher could take on, trusted guide.

Which is why you are a part of a movement. A movement to change the status quo, to insist that math is more than just rules and procedures to follow, and to challenge the idea that math is simple. We are a community of educators using our classrooms to reveal the joy that comes from tinkering with a problem and not rushing to get an instant answer. Together, we honor our students' learning processes by giving them the time and space to uncover the complexities and connections within mathematics.

You know all the time, sweat, and tears that go into building a classroom community of problem solvers. You understand that collaboration with others is vital to this movement so that together we can create something far greater together than we could alone. You are ready to do this work, for and with your students, for years to come.

In anticipation of the brilliant work I know you'll do, I want to express my gratitude. Thank you for reading this book and bringing its messages, strategies, and ideas to life in your classroom. Thank you for sharing these messages with your colleagues, so that our movement can grow and reach more classrooms of budding problem solvers. Thank you.

# References

Berger, Ron, et al. 2014. *Leaders of Their Own Learning: Transforming Schools Through Student-Engaged Assessment.* San Francisco, CA: Jossey-Bass.

Bishop, Rudine Sims. 1990. "Mirrors, Windows, and Sliding Glass Doors." *Perspectives: Choosing and Using Books for the Classroom* 6 (3): ix–xi.

Carpenter, Thomas P., et al. 2015. *Children's Mathematics: Cognitively Guided Instruction* (2nd ed.). Portsmouth, NH: Heinemann.

Dixon, Juli K., et al. 2018. *Making Sense of Mathematics for Teaching the Small Group.* Bloomington, IN: Solution Tree.

Freeman, Scott, et al. 2014. "Active Learning Increases Student Performance in Science, Engineering, and Mathematics." *Proceedings of the National Academy of Sciences of the United States of America* 111 (23): 8410–8415.

Hattie, John. 2009. *Visible Learning: A Synthesis of Over 800 Meta-Analyses Related to Achievement.* New York: Routledge.

Iehl, Mona. October 10, 2023. "Ambitious Teaching with Margaret 'Peg' Smith (No. 80)." MonaMath, Podcast. https://monamath.com/podcast/peg.

Michael, Joel. 2006. "Where's the Evidence that Active Learning Works?" *Advances in Physiology Education* 30 (4): 159–167.

National Council of Teachers of Mathematics (NCTM). 2014. *Principles to Actions: Ensuring Mathematical Success for All.* Reston, VA: National Council of Teachers of Mathematics.

National Governors Association Center for Best Practices and the Council of Chief State School Officers. 2010. "Standards for Mathematical Practice." https://www.thecorestandards.org/Math/Practice/.

National Research Council. 2015. *Adding It Up: Helping Children Learn Mathematics.* Washington, DC: The National Academies Press.

Seda, Pamela and Kyndall Brown. 2021. *Choosing to See: A Framework for Equity in the Math Classroom.* San Diego, CA: Dave Burgess Consulting.

Smith, Margaret S. and Mary Kay Stein. 2018. *5 Practices for Orchestrating Productive Mathematics Discussions* (2nd ed.). Reston, VA: National Council of Teachers of Mathematics.

The University of Chicago Consortium on School Research. 2017. "*The Role of Noncognitive Factors in Shaping School Performance.*" The

University of Chicago. https://consortium.uchicago.edu/sites/default/files/2018-11/The%20Role%20of%20Noncognitive-Aug2017-Consortium.pdf.

Zager, Tracy Johnston. 2017. *Becoming the Math Teacher You Wish You'd Had: Ideas and Strategies from Vibrant Classrooms*. Portland, ME: Stenhouse Publishers.

# Index

Page numbers in *italics* refer to figures.

## A

accuracy, clarity, and precision 66–8, 103–5
adaptive reasoning 29, *30*, 31
anchor charts: active listening *122*; feedback 147, *148*; grapple time 62, *63*, 66; participation in discussions 132
answer statement 103

## B

behavior as communication 87–8
Berger, R. et al. 28
Bishop, Dr. R. S. 171
brainstorm/brain dump *24*, 25, 125

## C

calling on next speaker 117–18
campfires analogy for discussion 114, *115*
caretaker role of teacher 120
check for understanding 49–50, 53
checklists: feedback 148–9; revising a word problem 163
circle up 117
clarity, accuracy and precision 66–8, 103–5
coach role of teacher 120
cold calls 119
collaboration 97
communication: behavior as 87–8; critical skills 113–14
community: math 20–7; of problem-solvers 6–7
conceptual understanding 29, *30*, 31
conferences 79–81, 89
confidence-building: and curiosity 186–8; independence and 45–6; and routine 16
conjectures: and generalizations 128–9; proving 140
connections 6, 106; questions, and sticky spots 176–7, 180
context of problem 44–5, 171
coordinator role of teacher 120
critical communication skills 113–14
curiosity 5, 69, 75, 121, 132; and confidence, tools to inspire 186–8
curriculum, use of 161–3, 181

## D

data and observations 177–8
deep dive 126–7
deep learning 5
deep reflections 145–6
discussion 38–9, 111–13; campfires analogy 114, *115*; common questions from teachers 130–2; facilitating for deeper understanding 120–3; facilitating engagement in 117–20; framework 123–9; goals of 114; good/strong 115–16; importance of 113–14
Dixon, J. et al. 71
doing the math, planning by 171–9

## E

equations, matching problem and strategy 101–3
errors *see* mistakes
expectations, setting 62
expertise of students 5, 47–8, 52; context of problem 44–5, 171
exploring an idea 125–6

## F

familiar and intentional problem-solving routine 14–18
feedback 147–9
five steps 14, 31–41; *see also specific steps*
forecasting/Forecasting Guides 172–3, 175–80; examples 35, 77, 157–8; need for 182; notes 89, 94
formative assessment 150–1

## G

generalizations 128–9
goals: learning 158–61, 179; setting 146–7; *see also specific steps*
grapple time 33–7, 54–5, 57–8; common questions from teachers 86–9; facilitating productive struggle 68–75; Forecasting Guide 177; four moves to facilitate thinking 75–86; goals of 60; grows mathematicians 59–60; pathway to sense-making 58–9; preparing for 60–8
growth mindset 25–6

## H

heads together 120

## I

Iehl, M. 159
independence, building 45–6
index cards 139, 145–6
intentional and familiar problem-solving routine 14–18
intentional number choice 169, *170*

## J

"just in case" and "just in time" scaffolds 71
just-right support 50–1, 53

## L

launch 31–3, 43–4; building independence 45–6; common questions from teachers 53–5; goals of 45; plan 46–53; student preparation 44–5
learning goals 158–61, 179
learning strategies and progressions 174–5
listening/listeners: students 98, 105–6; teachers 106–7, 121, *122*

## M

materials, preparing 180
math community 20–7
math conferences 79–81, 89
math norms 24–5
math proficiency, building 29–31
math progressions and learning strategies 174–5
math survey, as relationship building tool 22–4
mathematical discourse 5
mathematicians: becoming 18–20; grapple time 59–60; self-reflection habits 141–3
metacognition 113
mindset 25–6
mistakes: detection 106; reframing 26; rescuing students 64–5; sharing strategies with 107–8; as stepping stones 61–2
mix and mingle to build relationships 21
models and strategies 173
moves to facilitate thinking 75–86

## N

National Council of Teachers of Mathematics (NCTM) 64–5
National Research Council: *Add It Up* report 29

neutral role of teacher 69–70
"no erasing" norm 26
noncognitive factors 141
norms: discussions 132; math 24–5; "no erasing" 26
notice aloud 55, 87
nudge vs nugget 71–5

## O

observations: and data 177–8; math conferencing 79–80
one more problem, strategy for reflection 137–9, 150, 151
open-ended questions 80, 123, 131
ownership of learning 5, 27–9

## P

participation in discussions 132
patterns in questioning 122–3
physical, visual and symbolic models of strategy 173, *174*
planning 154–8; by doing the math 171–9; choosing a word problem 161–71; common questions from teachers 181–2; establishing a learning goal 158–61; launch 46–53; next problem 149–51; prep period 179–80
positive self-talk 26–7
precision, clarity, and accuracy 66–8, 103–5
prep period 179–80
problem choice and sources 180, 181–2
problem types 163–9
procedural fluency 29, *30*, 31
productive disposition 29, *30*, 31
productive struggle: for deep learning 5; facilitating 68–75; vs unproductive struggle 60–1, 86–7
progressions and learning strategies 174–5
prompts: deep dive 127; math conferencing 80
proving a conjecture 140

## Q

questions: answer statement 103; connections, and sticky spots 176–7, 180; discussions 122–3; math conferencing 79, 80; open-ended 80, 123, 131; teacher *see specific steps*
quick checks 143–5

## R

read alouds 9, 52, 53–4
read and retell 48–9, 52
reading support 53–4

reflection 39–41, 134–6; action taker 152–3; common questions from teachers 151–2; on feedback 147–9; goals of 137; planning next problem 149–51; self-reflection 140–7; to synthesize learning 137–40; as vital to learning 136
reframing mistakes 26
rehearsal time 124
relationship building 21, 22–4
relationship-focused strategies 87–8
resistance to reflection 152
revising a word problem 161–3
revising work 139
revoicing 119
routine, familiar and intentional problem-solving 14–18

## S

scanning 76
scribe role of teacher 98–105
Seda, P. and Brown, K. 16
self-reflection 140–7
self-talk, positive 26–7
sense of pride 118
sense-making pathway 58–9
sentence stems 130
sharing 37–8, 91–2; common questions from teachers 107–9; goals of 92; maintaining engagement during 105–7; norms 25; positions for 97–9; preparing space 93; scribe for 99–105; selection 93–7
showing math thinking 65–8
Smith, M. S. 158–9; and Stein, M. K. 172
Standards for Mathematical Practice 19, *20*
sticky spots, connections, questions and 176–7, 180
strategic competence 29, *30*, 31
strategies and models 173
structures and routines 17–18
stuckness, strategies for solving 86–7, 108–9
student roles: discussions 116, 118; grapple time *64*, 65
student strategies *see* forecasting/Forecasting Guides
student-centered instruction 5, 27–9

support 5; "just in case" and "just in time" 71; just-right 50–1, 53; math conferencing 81, 89; reading 53–4
symbolic, visual, and physical models of strategy 173, *174*
synthesizing learning 137–40

## T

teacher roles: discussions 116, 120–3; grapple time 64–5; scribe 98–105; *see also* support
telling the story 46–7, 52
think alouds 28, 152
thinking: four moves to facilitate 75–86; showing 65–8
thumbs up signal 117–18
time issues: discussions 119, 124; reflection 139, 143–5, 151; sharing 88–9, 109
turn and talk 38–9; deep dive 126–7; launch 43, 44; listening in 121; rehearsal time 124; sharing 109; and whole-group discussion 9, 10–11, 12, 131

## U

understanding 5, 6; check for 49–50, 53; conceptual 29, *30*, 31; facilitating deeper 120–3
University of Chicago's Consortium on School Research 141
unproductive vs productive struggle 60–1, 86–7

## V

visual, physical, and symbolic models of strategy 173, *174*

## W

walking 76–7
weekly schedule 14–15
"what did they say?" game 119
wrapping up vs trailing off 129

## Z

Zager, T. 60
zoning in 77–9

For Product Safety Concerns and Information please contact our EU
representative GPSR@taylorandfrancis.com
Taylor & Francis Verlag GmbH, Kaufingerstraße 24, 80331 München, Germany

www.ingramcontent.com/pod-product-compliance
Lightning Source LLC
Chambersburg PA
CBHW080924300426
44115CB00018B/2934